The Open University

centre for
MODERN LANGUAGES

OUVERTURE

Cadences   Livre 2
Le temps libre et le temps plein

L120 course team

OU team

Ghislaine Adams (*course manager*)
Marie-Claude Bovet (*course secretary*)
Joan Carty (*liaison librarian*)
Ann Cobbold (*course secretary*)
Jonathan Davies (*design group co-ordinator*)
Tony Duggan (*project controller*)
Jane Duffield (*project controller*)
Kevin Firth (*team member/author*)
Janis Gilbert (*graphic artist*)
David Hare (*team member/author*)
Pam Higgins (*designer*)
Angela Jamieson (*BBC producer*)
Marie-Noëlle Lamy (*course team chair/author*)
Kate Laughton (*editor*)
Mike Levers (*photographer*)
Ruth McCracken (*course manager*)
Reginald Melton (*IET*)
Hélène Mulphin (*team member/author*)
Jenny Ollerenshaw (*team member/author*)
Margaret Selby (*course secretary*)
Anne Stevens (*reading member*)
Betty Talks (*BBC series producer*)
Penny Vine (*BBC producer*)

External assessor

Professor Samuel Taylor (Department of French, University of St Andrews)

External consultants

Authors who contributed to the writing of the materials were: Martyn Bird; Elspeth Broady; Lucile Ducroquet; Brigitte Guénier; Philip Handley; Rod Hares; Hélène Lewis; Margaret Mitchell; Sandra Truscott; Margaret Tuccori.

Critical readers were: Lucette Barbarin; Malcolm Bower; Brian Page; John Pettit; Pam Shakespeare; Richard Tuffs. Bob Powell was the language adviser.

Supplementary picture and text research by Pierrick Picot. Proofs read by Danièle Bourdais.

Developmental testing

The course team would like to thank all those people involved in testing the course materials. Their comments have been invaluable in the preparation of the course. In particular, thanks go to the following members of IET:
Beryl Crooks; Ellie Chambers; Barbara Hodgson; Reginald Melton; Kay Pole; Don Whitehead; Alan Woodley; Hussein Zand.

The team would also like to thank the following adult education tutors: Liz Moss; Adèle Skegg; Theresa Young.

The Open University, Walton Hall, Milton Keynes MK7 6AA

First published 1994. Reprinted 1995; 1996; 1997

Edited, designed and typeset by the Open University

Printed in the United Kingdom by Butler and Tanner

ISBN 0 7492 6280 X

This text forms part of an Open University course. If you would like a copy of *Studying with the Open University* or more information on Open University language materials, please write to the Course Enquiries Data Service, P.O. Box 625, The Open University, Dane Road, Milton Keynes MK1 1TY.

1.5
L120-L500cad2i1.5

Contents

Introduction

In this book you will encounter a wide variety of people – from soldiers to students, bakers to monks – talking about their leisure interests and their working routines. In the first section, *La ronde des loisirs*, various people describe their leisure activities and explain why they enjoy what they do. The next section, *Les loisirs chez soi*, concentrates on pastimes centred on the home. In particular, you will meet a keen collector and see an enthusiastic cook making one of his favourite recipes. In contrast, the final section, *Le travail au quotidien*, deals with people's working lives and what they think of their jobs.

As you work through the sections, you will build on the work you did in Book 1 of *Cadences* by going over some basic grammar and vocabulary. You will learn to talk about how you spend your own time and practise and develop the four skills of listening, speaking, reading and writing.

On the Feature Cassette associated with this book you will meet members of an amateur theatre troupe, hear them explain what they love about putting on plays in their spare time and listen to them rehearsing a farce. You can listen to this cassette at any time during your study of this book.

1 La ronde des loisirs

STUDY CHART

	Topic	Activity/timing	Audio/video	Key points
1hr 10 mins	1.1 Que faites-vous de votre temps libre?	1 (5 mins)		Vocabulary: sports and hobbies
		2 (15 mins)	Video	
		3 (10 mins)		Using *du, de la* and *des*
		4 (20 mins)		Writing a postcard
45 mins	1.2 Marcher pour le plaisir	5 (15 mins)		Vocabulary: walking
		6 (5 mins)		
		7 (15 mins)	Audio	Justifying a choice
1 hr 10 mins	1.3 S'échapper des villes	8 (10 mins)	Audio	Vocabulary: indoor/outdoor sports activities
		9 (15 mins)	Audio	Understanding directions
		10 (5 mins)	Audio	Vocabulary: cycling
		11 (5 mins)	Audio	Recognizing 'filler' words
		12 (5 mins)	Audio	Using 'filler' words
		13 (5 mins)	Audio	Recognizing dropped syllables in speech
		14 (5 mins)	Audio	
2 hrs	1.4 Vos loisirs dans notre région	15 (15 mins)		Finding out information from a tourist guide entry
		16 (15 mins)	Audio	Describing and evaluating local facilities
		17 (10 mins)		Finding out information from two brochures
		18 (5 mins)		Preparing for writing
		19 (10 mins)		Recognizing links in writing
		20 (15 mins)		Writing about change in your own leisure activities
		21 (30 mins)	Audio	Section revision

*L*a ronde des loisirs, like *la ronde des desserts* (selection of desserts) which you find on the menu of some restaurants in France, offers a choice of many different leisure pursuits. The first topic in this section, *Que faites-vous de votre temps libre?,* takes a general look at what people do in their spare time. In *Marcher pour le plaisir* we focus on a particular activity – rambling – and then listen to some people explaining what they do to get away from it all in *S'échapper des villes*. Finally, in *Vos loisirs dans notre région*, we consider how to extract information from brochures to help organize leisure time/ holidays and we look at how leisure activities have changed over the years.

As you work through this section, you will review some basic grammar, learn how to describe your leisure activities and give reasons for choosing them. In addition, you will start work on developing your writing skills.

1.1 Que faites-vous de votre temps libre?

What do the French do with their leisure time? We asked a small sample of people to tell us what their hobbies were. As you will see and hear, our interviewees are fairly active, practising hobbies which fall into two categories: sports, and social or cultural pursuits. The video sequence featuring these interviews and the written exercise later in this topic will give you the vocabulary and the grammar you need to describe your own leisure activities.

Using 'du', 'de la' and 'des'

Talking about hobbies involves using *du, de la* and *des* before the names of the activities you want to describe and these words have to be chosen appropriately. We expect that you will have come across them before, but if you need to remind yourself how to use them accurately, pages 21–2 of the Grammar Book will tell you what the forms are, and page 219 shows you how to use them with expressions of quantity. As you work through this course book, it would also be a good idea to make a note in your dossier of all the hobbies and sports that interest you, grouping them according to whether *du, de la* or *des* precedes them.

Your first task is a vocabulary exercise, to familiarize you with some of the language of sports and hobbies which you will meet in this section.

Activité 1
5 MINUTES

1 Look at the list below. Write down what these words and phrases mean in English. If you don't already know them, try to guess their meaning, using a dictionary only as a last resort. *Du, de la* and *des* are in bold type.

Vérifiez le sens des expressions suivantes.

(a) faire **de la** voile

(b) faire **de la** natation

(c) faire **du** footing

(d) faire **de l'**équitation

(e) faire **de la** musculation

(f) faire **de la** planche à voile

(g) faire **de la** course

(h) lire **des** bandes dessinées

(i) pêcher

2 Check your answers in the *Corrigés* before continuing.

Vérifiez vos réponses avant de continuer.

The first video sequence is very brief and features Marie-Noëlle, a yoga teacher, Brother Marc, a Trappist monk, and Éric and Stéphane, two soldiers. They are all asked the same question: *Que faites-vous de votre temps libre?* (As you may remember from Book 1 of *Cadences*, asking a question by switching the order of subject and verb is a suitable technique for a slightly formal situation, as here in a filmed interview.) You are going to find out how different their hobbies are, and when they like to do them.

Activité 2
15 MINUTES
VIDEO

1 Read through the list of sports and activities below.

Lisez la liste d'activités sportives et de loisirs ci-dessous.

(a) footing

(b) cinéma

(c) sport

(d) tennis

(e) lire

(f) je sors

(g) je vais dans des cafés

(h) je vais dans des discothèques

(i) je regarde la télévision

2 Watch the four video interviews in *Que faites-vous de votre temps libre?* (19:35–20:46) and tick each sport/activity whenever you hear it mentioned. (When an activity is mentioned a second or third time, it may be phrased slightly differently.)

Regardez la séquence vidéo et cochez les noms de ces loisirs à chaque fois que vous les entendez.

Pour vous aider

pratiquer   to do (a slightly more formal synonym for *faire du* or *de la*; e.g. *pratiquer la voile* is to go sailing on a regular basis)

autrement   otherwise

je n'hésite pas à... lire   I don't think twice about reading

pour me déconnecter de   to disengage my mind from

des choses... qui me passionnent   things which I find fascinating (*or* really exciting things)

3   *Répondez en anglais aux questions suivantes.*

(a)   What is the main difference between the two soldiers' life styles?

(b)   How does Brother Marc justify his choice of reading matter?

4   Watch the video sequence again. Who made the following comments about the timing of their leisure schedules?

Regardez de nouveau la séquence vidéo. Qui donne les précisions suivantes?

(a)   régulièrement

(b)   quand j'ai des loisirs

(c)   quand je suis fatigué

(d)   tous les soirs

Who gave no such indications?

Quelle personne n'a pas donné de précisions?

en passant » » » »

You already know *bien* as the translation for 'well'. In the video sequence you've just watched, Stéphane uses *bien* with a different meaning. Like 'did' or 'do' in English, *bien* emphasizes what has just been said: *'je fais un peu de sport – j'ai bien dit, un peu de sport'*. This could be translated as: 'I do a bit of sport, and I do mean a bit' or 'I do a bit of sport, as I say, a bit'. Here are other ways of using *bien* with this meaning:

> *Tu as bien dit 'rendez-vous à huit heures'?*
> You did say 'Let's meet at eight', didn't you?

> *Mais oui, j'ai bien fermé le gaz!*
> Yes, I switched the gas off!

Note the position of *bien* between the two parts of the verb. If the verb had only one part, *bien* would appear in the following position:

> *Je vois bien que tu es fatigué.*
> I can (easily) see that you are tired.

» » » »

In the next *activité* the emphasis is on using *du, de la* or *des* accurately when writing about your own leisure activities.

Activité 3
10 MINUTES

Write down one sentence for each of your own pastimes, using the verb *faire* and re-using the phrases which you have met so far if they apply to you. If your hobbies are different, look up their names in your dictionary. (You will need to note their gender in order to know whether to use *du, de la* or *des*.)

Décrivez vos loisirs comme dans le modèle (une phrase pour chaque passe-temps).

> *Exemple*
>
> | | |
> |---|---|
> | Say what you do | Je fais du volley ball… |
> | And when or how often you do it | … tous les samedis. |

Keep your answers to this *activité* handy, as you will need them for *Activité 4*.

Writing to friends

Writing even a simple message involves linking sentences smoothly. When you worked on postcards in Book 1 of *Cadences* you learned how to begin and end your message. Now you're going to focus on linking the sentences inside the text. In English, as in French, words like 'but' (*mais*), 'so' (*donc*), 'for instance' (*par exemple*) introduce new topics, while also creating in the reader's mind a link with the ideas that have already been mentioned. The connection can be established through a contrast (*mais*), a logical consequence (*donc*), an illustration (*par exemple*), or in other ways. Whatever the nature of the link, the effect of connecting parts of the message in this way is to make your writing style much more fluid. The next *activité* will give you chance to try this out and then, perhaps, you will want to send a message to a friend. Remember, he or she doesn't have to be French or in France to appreciate receiving a letter in French!

In *Activité 4* a young woman, Noémi, finds a few minutes to write a card to her friend Julia. We want you to use her postcard as a model to write one of your own. You may need to alter some or all of the details: your hobbies, family circumstances and routines may be different. You could also adapt Noémi's closing remark to express slightly different sentiments: *Ici il fait beau et j'espère qu'il en est de même pour vous/Nous sommes en bonne santé et nous espérons qu'il en est de même pour vous.* A quick look at the postcard exercise in Section 1 of *Cadences*, Book 1, will help to remind you how to modify a model text and how to begin and end your card.

Activité 4
20 MINUTES

1 *Lisez la carte de Noémi à son amie Julia.*

Chère Julia,
Un petit bonjour de Londres.
Depuis mon retour de vacances,
je suis très prise par mon travail.
Mais j'ai quand même décidé de
m'occuper de moi! Par exemple, je
fais du badminton une fois par
semaine, et je chante dans une cho-
-rale tous les vendredis soirs. Et
puis de temps en temps, je me
réserve un petit week-end pour aller
voir des amis à la campagne.
    Tout ça fait beaucoup d'activités,
même un peu trop! Mais autrement
tout va bien, le moral est bon. J'es-
-père qu'il en est de même pour toi.
    Je t'embrasse,
        Noémi

Julia Pernel
8, cours Druault
Lormeaux
    84160

Pour vous aider

quand même all the same

m'occuper de moi put time aside for myself

le moral est bon I'm in good spirits

j'espère qu'il en est de même pour toi I hope the same goes for you

2 Underline the three phrases in the postcard which express how frequently Noémi does things.

Soulignez les trois expressions de fréquence de la carte postale.

3 Circle each link phrase in the second paragraph.

Encerclez les trois expressions qui relient les éléments du deuxième paragraphe.

4 Now write a postcard to someone you know using as much or as little of the original phrasing as you need in order to describe your own leisure activities. In the example overleaf we have emboldened phrases for you to re-use or adapt if possible. You'll need to decide whether you're writing to a woman or to a man, and whether your relationship with this person is such that you should use *tu* (for good friends or relatives) or *vous* (for acquaintances).

Écrivez une carte postale à une personne de votre choix. Réutilisez ou adaptez les mots en caractères gras.

Chère Julia,

Un petit bonjour de **Londres**.

Depuis mon retour de vacances, je suis très prise par mon travail. Mais j'ai quand même décidé de m'occuper de moi! Par exemple, je fais du badminton **une fois par semaine**, et je chante dans une chorale **tous les vendredis soirs**. Et puis **de temps en temps**, je me réserve un petit week-end pour aller voir des amis à la campagne.

Tout ça fait beaucoup d'activités, même un peu trop! **Mais autrement tout va bien, le moral est bon. J'espère qu'il en est de même pour toi**.

Je t'embrasse

Noémi

Before moving on to the next topic, make sure that you know how to use *du, de la* and *des* and complete your dossier work on this if necessary.

1.2 Marcher pour le plaisir

In recent years, interest in walking for pleasure has been on the increase in France and you're now going to read an extract from a magazine article about the joys of rambling. It describes when people took up walking as a pastime, and why.

Activité 5

15 MINUTES

1   *Lisez le texte suivant.*

Pour Agnès, petit bout de femme de 36 ans qui vit à Paris, 'la randonnée est le meilleur moyen de renouer contact avec la nature, d'apprécier un autre rythme de vie'. Et c'est l'occasion de retrouver le vrai goût des choses: 'Après 20 km de marche sous le soleil, la poire que l'on déguste les pieds dans l'eau a une toute autre saveur!' s'exclame-t-elle la mine gourmande. Patrick, 40 ans, médecin généraliste, a commencé à randonner alors qu'il était étudiant. Il n'avait pas de gros moyens financiers; la marche à pied lui permettait de passer de vraies vacances à moindres frais. 'C'est une façon idéale de décompresser après les examens'...

André Pilet, septuagénaire, féru de botanique, a redécouvert la randonnée depuis une trentaine d'années... Son prochain objectif est de rallier, à l'automne prochain, le cirque de Gavarnie à partir du Portugal. Principal moteur d'André: le bonheur de partager avec ses compagnons de route joies et souffrances, et de découvrir de nouveaux horizons...

Maurice, 69 ans, n'a jamais fait de longue randonnée. Deux heures de promenade, une à deux fois par semaine, suffisent à son bonheur. 'C'est une détente. Je me retrouve seul avec mes pensées et je m'absorbe dans la contemplation de la nature.'

(*Pèlerin Magazine*, 19 juin 1992, pp. 18–19)

Pour vous aider

petit bout de femme   tiny slip of a woman

la randonnée   rambling (if in upland area, hill walking; can also refer to exploring on a bicycle, a horse or in a canoe)

sous le soleil   in the sun (also *au soleil*)

l'on déguste   you savour

la mine gourmande   with a look that says 'this is going to be really delicious'

la marche à pied   walking (general term, in town or country)

à moindres frais   less expensively

féru de   very keen on

le cirque de Gavarnie   valley in the Pyrenees, a favourite spot for walkers

rallier le cirque de Gavarnie à partir du Portugal   to get to the cirque de Gavarnie, having started off in Portugal

partager   to share

souffrances   sufferings

une détente   a way of relaxing

n'a jamais fait de longue randonnée   has never done any long-distance rambling

2 Write down in English the answers to the following questions.

Notez en anglais les réponses aux questions suivantes.

(a) What three reasons does Agnès give for enjoying rambling?

(b) What two reasons does Patrick give for taking up this activity?

3 Find the French for the following expressions.

Trouvez l'équivalent français des expressions suivantes.

(a) When he was a student.

(b) He didn't have a lot of money.

(c) It's the ideal way to unwind.

(d) In the last thirty years or so.

Activité 6

5   MINUTES

A specialist magazine for ramblers, *Marcher de 7 à 87 ans*, wants to improve its coverage and has designed a questionnaire to elicit information about its readers' tastes. Respondents to the survey will be sent a free ordnance survey map (*une carte d'état-major*). Imagine you are Maurice, the sixty-nine-year-old man described in the text you have just read, and fill in the questionnaire opposite.

La revue 'Marcher de 7 à 87 ans' s'adresse à des lecteurs qui font de la randonnée. Elle propose un questionnaire à ses lecteurs. Vous êtes Maurice et vous répondez au questionnaire ci-contre.

If you want to revise the work you have already done on how to ask questions, have a look at the way the questions are phrased in the questionnaire. Re-read the explanations given in Section 2 of *Cadences*, Book 1, if necessary.

Also, if you have time, and if you need to, you could use the description of Agnès and her fellow ramblers as a basis for revising your work on past tenses. The end of the first paragraph of the text illustrates the imperfect employed to explain something which used to happen. The last two paragraphs provide two examples of past participles: *André... a redécouvert la randonnée* and *Maurice... n'a jamais fait de longue randonnée*. This is a good time to check that you still know how to form a past participle (see Section 2 of *Cadences*, Book 1, if necessary).

Randonneur, qui êtes-vous?

CADEAU
Pour les dix premiers lecteurs qui répondent à ce questionnaire : une carte d'état-major de votre région préférée!

1 Quel type de randonnée pratiquez-vous? (plusieurs réponses possibles)

❏ pédestre
❏ équestre
❏ cyclotouriste
❏ canoë
❏ autre

2 Combien de fois pratiquez-vous votre type de randonnée dans l'année?

❏ moins de 5 fois
❏ entre 5 et 10 fois
❏ entre 10 et 50 fois
❏ plus de 50 fois

3 Quelle durée de randonnée préférez-vous?

❏ quelques heures
❏ 1 jour
❏ 2 jours
❏ 5 jours
❏ 7 jours
❏ 10 jours et plus

4 Préférez-vous partir:

❏ seul?
❏ en famille?
❏ avec un guide?
❏ avec une association?

5 Dans vos randonnées, quel type d'équipement emportez-vous?

❏ jumelles
❏ appareil-photo
❏ skis
❏ magnétophone
❏ matériel de camping
❏ produits pour bronzer

6 Qu'est-ce qui vous plaît particulièrement dans notre revue?

	oui	non
les suggestions de promenade	❏	❏
les articles sur la nature	❏	❏
les informations sur les safaris	❏	❏
notre page «destinations lointaines»	❏	❏
nos listes d'auberges de jeunesse	❏	❏
nos adresses gastronomiques	❏	❏

Justifying a choice

In Book 1 of *Cadences* you practised using *parce que* to give reasons. But there are many other ways in which you can justify a choice. For example, as you saw in the text about ramblers, you can say why you've chosen something and what opportunities it presents. Agnès appreciated the opportunity (*l'occasion*) to rediscover the true taste of things:

> C'est l'occasion de…

Other ways of saying why something is the best option are:

> C'est le meilleur moyen de…

> C'est une façon idéale de…

You can also reinforce the whole idea by stressing that it's **your** opinion:

> Je trouve que c'est…

> D'après moi, c'est…

You are now going to use the Activities Cassette for the first time in this book. You'll hear a conversation between Antony and Noémi. Noémi, unlike the ramblers, likes to do her sport in a sports hall (*un gymnase*). Here Noémi is justifying her choice of badminton as a way to relax. You'll listen to her first and then practise justifying something you like to do. We have given you some of the phrases you might need.

Activité 7

15 MINUTES

AUDIO 1

1   Listen to the conversation between Antony and Noémi. Concentrate on the two reasons Noémi gives for taking up badminton, and on Antony's reason for agreeing to go along too.

Écoutez la conversation d'Antony et de Noémi. Remarquez que Noémi donne à Antony deux raisons de faire du badminton. Remarquez aussi pourquoi Antony accepte de jouer.

Pour vous aider

ça ne me dit rien   it doesn't appeal to me (*or* I don't feel like it)

je ne sais pas quoi choisir   I don't know what to choose

2   The phrase *c'est* occurs four times in this conversation, each time introducing a reason. Listen to the audio extract again and fill in the missing words in the following sentences. They are in the order in which you will hear them.

Remplissez les trous à la deuxième écoute.

(a) C'est _____ _____ _____ _____ _____

_____ .

(b) C'est _____ _____ _____ _____ .

(c) C'est _____ _____ _____ _____ _____

_____ .

(d) C'est _____ _____ s'_____ .

3   Now choose either an activity that you enjoy or one that you dislike and jot down reasons for your choice. We have given you some suggestions of the sorts of thing you could say. The *corrigé* gives you a couple of possible answers.

Choisissez une activité que vous aimez, ou au contraire une activité que vous n'aimez pas. Notez les raisons de votre choix.

Moi, quand je suis fatigué(e), j'aime…

À mon avis, c'est… (*or, alternatively,* Je trouve que c'est…)

Another possibility would be to say:

Le/la _____ , ça ne me dit rien parce que…

And here are some of the phrases which you might use to describe the circumstances:

- après les examens

- quand je suis en vacances en été

- quand je rentre le soir

- quand j'ai une heure de libre

If you use *faire* to describe what you like to do, remember to put *du, de la* or *des* before the noun, as appropriate.

4   Now say your reasons out loud or, if you wish, record yourself.

Donnez maintenant vos raisons à voix haute ou, si vous voulez, enregistrez-vous sur cassette.

1.3 S'échapper des villes

Even for those who haven't got the cirque de Gavarnie on the doorstep, there is a lot of pleasure to be gained from setting out on a bicycle and exploring the local area, particularly if you live in a town with easy access to the countryside. In this topic you will be listening to people who like to get away (*s'échapper*) from their jobs in town.

Extending your listening skills

We listen to people for many different reasons. For instance, sometimes we need to take in instructions or directions, and we rely on visual clues like a diagram or a map. Listening to a conversation is a different kind of process, during which we may be paying attention to what is being discussed or to more indirect information, for example the clues people are giving out about their own personalities and ways of relating to others.

As you work through this topic, you'll be listening for a variety of things: general information about someone's life style, the specific details of a cycling expedition and clues to the relationship between two speakers. You're also going to listen to a song and learn to spot how some French speakers drop syllables, a habit which goes some way towards explaining the impression that 'French people speak fast'.

You may find it easier if, at each stage in the listening process, you concentrate on what we have asked you to notice rather than trying to understand everything at once.

Finally, you'll also get chance to practise some of the phrases which you've been listening to, including the 'filler' words that play such an important part in keeping a conversation going.

La sportive

We start with Marie-Thérèse, an energetic town-dweller, who tells Marie-Lise what she does when she can get away (*quand je peux m'échapper*). Like Noémi, Marie-Thérèse uses a gym, which she calls *une salle*, short for *une salle de sport. En salle* can thus be translated as 'indoors'.

Activité 8
10 MINUTES

1 Play the audio extract, listening particularly for the leisure pursuits mentioned.

   Écoutez l'extrait et cherchez à reconnaître les loisirs mentionnés.

   Pour vous aider

   m'exercer to exercise

   un groupe de copines a group of women friends

   soit ... soit either ... or

   c'est assez vallonné it's rather hilly

2 Marie-Thérèse goes to the countryside for a few days. From what you know of her interests, tick the objects which she will be taking with her.

   Marie-Thérèse part à la campagne quelques jours. Qu'est-ce qu'elle emporte?

(a) un pantalon de golf ❏

(b) une pompe à bicyclette ❏

(c) une raquette de tennis ❏

(d) un maillot de bain ❏

(e) une lotion pour les pieds ❏

(f) des livres ❏

(g) des chaussons de danse ❏

3   Listen to Audio Extract 2 again, but this time think about clues which
    indicate that Marie-Thérèse and Marie-Lise know each other, though not
    very well. One clue is in the language used; the other in the content of
    the conversation. Explain what the clues are in English.

*Réécoutez toute la conversation entre Marie-Lise et Marie-Thérèse.
Qu'est-ce qui indique qu'elles se connaissent sans être amies intimes?*

De belles balades à faire

You're now going to imagine that you have an opportunity to spend a few
days, with a hired or borrowed bicycle, in a pleasant part of the French
countryside where there are nice rides to be had (*de belles balades à faire*).
(*Une balade* is a walk, a ride on a bicycle, or in a car, or even on a horse.
The vehicle doesn't matter, the idea of *balade* is that it is done at leisure and
for pleasure.) A friendly local person points out a particularly good cycle ride
for you to try. But can you understand the directions you are given?

Activité 9

1 5   M I N U T E S

A U D I O   3

39

1   Study the map overleaf and its key and then tick off the features listed
    below them when you've found where they are.

*Regardez bien la carte et la légende qui se trouvent à la page suivante,
pour trouver les repères mentionnés dessous. Cochez-les quand vous les
avez trouvés.*

2   Now listen to the directions given to you in Audio Extract 3 by Marie-Lise.
    As you listen, trace the route on the map with a pencil.

Écoutez l'extrait et tracez au crayon l'itinéraire recommandé.

Pour vous aider

ça en vaut la peine   it's worth it

vous avez une très très belle descente   there is a hill going down with a
    really beautiful view

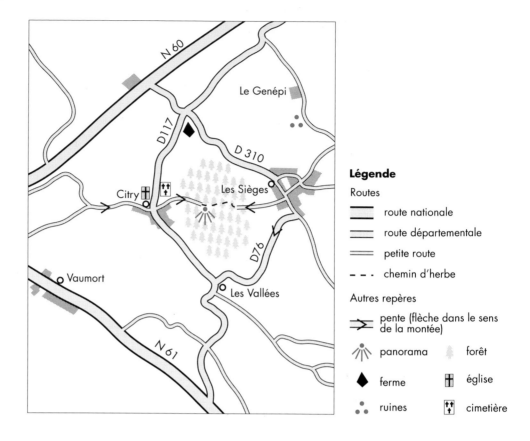

Légende

Routes

━━━ route nationale

▨▨▨ route départementale

═══ petite route

- - - chemin d'herbe

Autres repères

⟫ pente (flèche dans le sens de la montée)

⁂ panorama   🌲 forêt

◆ ferme   ✝ église

⁖ ruines   ⛪ cimetière

Pour vous aider

pente (flèche dans le sens de la montée)   slope
   (arrow points uphill)

Note that in France roads are classified as N
(*route nationale*) or D (*route départementale*).
The letter D or N and the appropriate number
appear on road signs, as well as on maps.

(a) le village appelé Les Sièges ❑

(b) le panorama ❑

(c) l'église ❑

(d) le cimetière ❑

(e) les deux départementales ❑

(f) la grosse ferme isolée ❑

Vélo tout terrain

In the next audio extract Guillaume explains where he likes to take his mountain bike, or VTT (*vélo tout terrain*). He mentions customs officers (*douaniers*) in connection with coastal paths. Before you listen, think for a moment about what that connection might be. You will then find it easier to understand the second half of Guillaume's explanations.

Activité 10

5   MINUTES

AUDIO   4

6 S

Listen to the audio extract while reading the following transcript.

Écoutez l'extrait et lisez la transcription ci-dessous.

Guillaume	Personnellement, ben… j'essaie de…, je pratique des activités, notamment (le) vélo tout terrain qui est une activité très très intéressante pour partager avec la nature, pour redécouvrir justement une vie très équilibrée, très saine.
Marie-Lise	Alors, vous sortez de Nantes, avec votre vélo?
Guillaume	Bien sûr, bien sûr!
Marie-Lise	Vous allez où?
Guillaume	Bien sûr, j'adore pratiquer le vélo tout terrain en bord de mer, c'est très paradoxal puisqu'on ne peut pas aller dans l'eau avec un vélo tout terrain, mais en tout cas les chemins de douaniers sont très très intéressants.
Marie-Lise	Les chemins quoi?
Guillaume	Douaniers.
Marie-Lise	Qu'est-ce que c'est que ça?
Guillaume	Vous ne connaissez pas?
Marie-Lise	Pas du tout.
Guillaume	Ben, les chemins douaniers, c'est les… les chemins par lesquels on pouvait surveiller les accès sur le littoral, et éviter que certaines personnes ne viennent déposer des… des marchandises… euh à des moments ou à des époques non autorisés.
Marie-Lise	Bien sûr, c'est, c'est, c'est sur la plage, alors?
Guillaume	C'est sur la plage, oui.
Marie-Lise	C'est du sable, ce chemin?
Guillaume	Ah, c'est du sable.
Marie-Lise	Et donc, vous pouvez… euh…
Guillaume	Pratiquer… euh, à la fois, les joies du vélo, dans un environnement maritime, c'est un paradoxe.

Helping the conversation flow

Guillaume, Marie-Thérèse and Marie-Lise all use some words as 'fillers', to help the flow of the conversation rather than to add meaning. For instance, in the previous transcript, the third time Guillaume spoke he started with *bien sûr*, but none of the meaning would have been lost if he hadn't said *bien sûr*. Words or phrases like *alors* (then), *bien sûr* (of course) and *eh bien* or *ben* (well) do not refer to specific ideas. This is not to say that they are always meaningless: compare the meaning of 'then' in 'And then (i.e. next) what did he do?' and in 'Come on then, let's go!', where you could omit 'then' and still retain the meaning. The same applies to *alors*: *Et alors, qu'est-ce qu'il a fait?* and *Bon, alors, allons-y*.

Notice too how Guillaume often repeats the last words he has heard. This way (probably without being aware of it) he provides continuity between Marie-Lise's remarks and his own. If you listen to an interview between two people in English, you'll find that this is a conversational technique shared by both cultures.

In *Activité 11* we have compiled a small collection of the 'filler' words used by Marie-Thérèse, Marie-Lise and Guillaume. When you listen to the audio extract, notice the intonation used, as you are going to imitate it when you do *Activité 12*.

Activité 11
5 MINUTES

AUDIO 5

9o.

Listen for the following words and phrases and tick each time you hear them. You should have nine ticks in all.

Cochez ces expressions chaque fois que vous les entendez. Vous cocherez neuf fois en tout.

- alors
- bien sûr
- eh bien (*or* bien *or* ben)

Activité 12
5 MINUTES

AUDIO 6

1o7

Listen to the four questions and answers on Audio Extract 6. Repeat each answer in the gap that has been left, imitating the intonation (don't be afraid to exaggerate *bien sûr*).

Écoutez les quatre questions et réponses de l'Extrait 6. Répétez les quatre réponses pendant les pauses. Imitez bien l'intonation.

Question	Vous allez sur la plage avec votre vélo?
Antony	Bien sûr, bien sûr!
Question	C'est des plages de quoi, dans la région de Nantes?

Antony	Ben, des plages de sable.
Question	Et vous faites du sport tous les week-ends?
Antony	Eh bien, quand je peux, en tout cas.
Question	Et si le temps est mauvais?
Antony	Alors, je reste chez moi!

Coping with dropped syllables in speech

French people in most of the northern half of France tend to drop the [ə] sound in phrases like *je t'ai vu* (I saw you). The remaining sounds are then run together, resulting in something like *j't'ai vu*, so [ʒətɛvy] becomes [ʒtɛvy]. This makes their speech faster and more difficult to understand. However, as the habit is very prevalent, it's a good idea to practise recognizing this when you hear it.

The next two *activités* will help you do so. You can guess the meaning of *me remettre en forme* if you remember *c'est une façon idéale de rester en forme*, which you met in *Activité 7*.

Activité 13

5   MINUTES

 **AUDIO   7**

This audio extract contains five pairs of sentences. Some of the pairs are pronounced identically; others differ because syllables have been dropped. Listen to the extract and put a tick against those pairs which are pronounced the same.

Cochez les expressions qui sont prononcées de façon identique.

Phrases (a) and (b)
Je vais refaire de la voile.   ☑ ✗

Phrases (c) and (d)
Je prends le train lundi.   ❏

Phrases (e) and (f)
Tiens, voilà le menu de la crêperie.   ❏

Phrases (g) and (h)
Je dois me remettre en forme.   ❏   ✗

Phrases (i) and (j)
C'est le meilleur moyen de se détendre.   ❏   ✗

Activité 14
5 MINUTES

A U D I O 8

137

This audio extract contains part of a well-known nursery rhyme. It means, roughly, 'Let's go for a walk in the woods while the wolf is not there. If the wolf were there, it would eat us, but as it isn't, it won't!' As you listen to the extract, look at the pairs of phrases below and tick the phrase which you hear.

Écoutez l'extrait de la chanson et cochez l'expression entendue.

promenons-nous ☐
prom'nons-nous ☐

il nous mangerait ☐
il nous mang'rait ☐

il nous mangera pas ☐
il nous mang'ra pas ☐

en passant » » » »

The rest of the song is a dialogue between the children and the wolf – who was there after all! Each time the children chorus *'Loup y es-tu? Entends-tu? Que fais-tu?'*, the wolf replies *'Je mets ma chemise'*, *'Je mets mon chapeau'* and so on with every item of clothing. Depending on the imagination of the singer taking the part of the wolf, the list can be quite extensive! The end is always the same, however: the wolf shouts *'Et je viens vous manger!'* as the children all scream with terror and delight.

» » » »

1.4 Vos loisirs dans notre région

This topic is about finding your way around a guide book or brochure and discovering what is available by way of amenities and organized pursuits. We begin by looking at choice of accommodation and courses suitable for people wishing to pursue various sporting activities. Then we focus on fishing, looking at fishing enthusiasts at the turn of the century and now.

As you work through the topic, you will practise reading documents for information and writing continuous prose. You will also revise the use of the imperfect.

The first two *activités* introduce you to the language of regional tourism and you will be choosing which of two gîtes you would prefer to stay in.

en passant ▶ ▶ ▶ ▶

Un gîte rural est une maison, souvent installée dans une région touristique, qui est proposée aux visiteurs pour une ou plusieurs semaines, ou pour un week-end. Dans de nombreux gîtes, on est indépendant et on fait sa cuisine soi-même. Dans d'autres, la famille habite sur place, ou pas très loin. Les propriétaires font le petit déjeuner et parfois le repas (table d'hôte). Il existe aussi des gîtes d'enfants, pour les enfants des villes pendant les vacances scolaires. Un gîte peut recevoir entre six et onze enfants. Une famille qui reçoit plus de six enfants est aidée par un animateur. Passer quelques jours dans un gîte rural, c'est une des meilleures façons de pratiquer des loisirs dans la campagne française.

▶ ▶ ▶ ▶

Activité 15
15 MINUTES

1 Overleaf are adverts for two gîtes. Read them and the key carefully, then use the words in the box to complete the following description.

Lisez attentivement les descriptions des gîtes qui se trouvent à la page suivante. Étudiez la légende, puis insérez dans le texte les mots de l'encadré ci-dessous.

Jouarre, c'est joli, mais malheureusement la voiture est

_____ . C'est un peu moins _____ qu'à

Vincelles, mais il n'y a pas grand-chose à faire. L'avantage, quand même,

c'est que le coin est très _____ . Et puis la maison est

_____ , donc il n'y a pas de propriétaire sur place. Il habite à

douze kilomètres du gîte.

> cher, indépendante, indispensable, calme

Pour vous aider
il n'y a pas grand-chose à faire   there isn't a lot to do
le coin   the area (informal)
sur place   on the spot

Jouarre

Ouvert toute l'année

1 chambre d'hôtes dans une maison totalement indépendante avec grand jardin, 1 chambre de 2 pers. avec salle de bains particulière. Salle de séjour, salon à la disposition des hôtes. Mer, plage, pêche (12 km). Restaurant (7km). Voiture indispensable.

Prix: 145 F 2 pers. lit suppl enfant : 45 F

Vincelles

À la ferme

3 chambres d'hôtes situées dans la même maison que le logement du propriétaire, 2 chambres de 2 pers. et 1 chambre de 3 pers. avec salle de bains commune. Chauffage central. Pêche (3 km) – piscine, équitation, tennis, location de vélos, chemins pédestres (4 km) – mer, plage, voile (6 km).

Prix: 200 F 1 pers. 250 F 2 pers. 300 F 3 pers.

Légende

 Pêche

 Équitation

 Rivière, lac, mer, plage

 Baignade

 Piscine couverte ou découverte

 Voile

 Tennis

2   Tick which of the two gîtes you would prefer if you were like the people below. Explain your choice in English.

Cochez le gîte à recommander aux personnes ci-dessous. Expliquez votre choix en anglais.

(a) Vous adorez passer des heures dans le bain.

Vincelles   ❏

Jouarre   ❏

(b) Vous n'aimez pas avoir froid.

Vincelles   ❏

Jouarre   ❏

(c) Vous êtes un couple avec un enfant et vous n'avez pas de gros moyens financiers.

Vincelles   ❏

Jouarre   ❏

'Si' and 'oui'

In French *oui* is not the only word for 'yes'. If you answer 'yes' to a question put to you in the negative, you have to say *si*, not *oui*. For example:

– Tu **n**'as **pas** faim?

– **Si**, je n'ai rien mangé au petit déjeuner!

For more examples, see page 236 in the Grammar Book.

G

Activité 16
1 5   M I N U T E S

While you are spending a few days in a village called Saint-Potan, a friend telephones you to find out how you are enjoying it. Listen to the conversation and record your responses in the gaps after each English prompt. (Don't forget to use the word for 'a walk' which you learned from Marie-Lise's instructions in *Activité 9.*)

Répondez en français aux questions de l'extrait audio, d'après les suggestions en anglais.

Les alentours de Vallonne

When you are looking for things to do in an area of France, the first place to visit is the Syndicat d'Initiative, also called the Office du Tourisme, where you can pick up brochures, price lists, maps and timetables. Overleaf are extracts from two brochures for the area around (*les alentours de*) Vallonne, in particular the small towns of Parrigny and Saint-Savinien. The brochures give you practical information and tell you about the activities on offer.

Activité 17

10 MINUTES

1 Read both brochure extracts, then decide which town is most suitable for the people listed below. Explain your choice in English.

Quel est la ville qui répond le mieux aux besoins de ces personnes? Expliquez votre choix en anglais.

(a) A couple with children.

(b) An older couple.

(c) A single person.

À Saint-Savinien

LES PISCINES

Piscine municipale : boulevard de la Convention (ouverte tous les jours, solarium, sauna).
Club natation bébé à partir de 1 an : le samedi matin 10h à 10h30.
École de natation 5 à 8 ans : 16h30 à 18h30 tous les jours.

LES PLANS D'EAU

Valbeau : à 12 km sud de Saint-Savinien, 17 ha, équipement pour voile, planche à voile (location matériel), tél : mairie 6.87.07.45.

VOILE, PLANCHE À VOILE

Club de voile pour tous : avenue Boffrand, pointe sud de l'île,
M. Marchand, tél: 6.97.22.89, entraînement mars à novembre.

SKI NAUTIQUE

Le club Nautisme et Liberté : organise des stages de ski nautique avec 10% de réduction sur les cours collectifs pour les 14 à 18 ans.
Il est obligatoire de savoir nager.

LA PÊCHE

Si vous désirez pêcher en famille, vous pouvez vous adresser à l'association «Plaisir de l'eau» (5 avenue de la République). Cartes de pêche tarif réduit moins de 15 ans (15 F). Adulte (350 F). Valable 1 an.

Pour vous aider

à partir de   starting from

location   hiring (e.g. of a facility or a piece of equipment; but *la location d'un gîte* means renting a gîte)

entraînement   training

nager   to swim

À Parrigny

LE CHEVAL

Club hippique du domaine de Clairis (chevaux, hébergement, randonnées et stages).

Centre équestre de Cloiry (chevaux, stages, cours particuliers, hébergement individuel).

TENNIS

Tennis-club de Vaule : bar-restaurant, télévision. Stages d'été, école de tennis le mercredi après-midi : venez seul, nous vous trouvons un(e) partenaire de jeu. Abonnements saisonniers, location à l'heure. Prendre les inscriptions au Syndicat d'Initiative.

LA RANDONNÉE PÉDESTRE

Les amateurs de randonnée pédestre peuvent pratiquer leur sport favori en parcourant les nombreux sentiers de la région de Parrigny.
Vous pouvez aussi découvrir la forêt avec l'Office National des Forêts, de juin à septembre, tél : 6.46.30.33.

LES PARCOURS DE SANTÉ

Si vous aimez mieux la promenade de santé, le parcours de la Hariette donne aux moins jeunes l'occasion de marcher une petite heure sans fatigue.

Pour vous aider

cours particuliers private lessons
hébergement lodging (refers to being put up temporarily at a gîte or a holiday village)
abonnements pass (here, season's pass; un abonnement mensuel is a monthly pass)
prendre les inscriptions to enrol
si vous aimez mieux la promenade if you prefer walking
le parcours the route

2 Write at least two sentences in French to explain which town would suit you best, and why. You could follow the model below (but feel free to be more creative).

Et vous, vous préférez Saint-Savinien ou Parrigny? Expliquez pourquoi en une ou deux phrases selon le modèle ci-dessous.

Personnellement, je préfère aller dans la région de _____

parce qu'on peut _____ et que j'aime le/la

_____ .

Les pêcheurs

Fishing is a popular hobby among a wide cross-section of the French population. But it wasn't always so, as you'll discover by looking at photographs which show how it was 'then' and how it is 'now'. As you study the photographs and write a description of them, you'll learn how to contrast the past and present. You'll also be able to check that you can use the imperfect tense accurately in writing.

Building up vocabulary

When exploring a new area of vocabulary, don't forget that you can use your dictionary creatively. For instance, *la pêche* means fishing. Or is it angling? How do you say trout fishing? Or shrimping? The answer to all these is given in a single entry in your dictionary. If you look up the noun *pêche* (ignoring *pêche* meaning peach and selecting the fishing entry), you will find four different English words for *pêche* – fishing, angling, whaling and gathering. In French they are all *pêche*. The differences between them are expressed by *à la, au* or *aux*, followed by the type of animal or instrument used.

>*la pêche à la ligne*   fishing, angling (*une ligne* is a rod)
>
>*la pêche à la baleine*   whaling
>
>*la pêche aux moules*   gathering mussels

One of the secrets to building up vocabulary lies in reading the 'small print' in the dictionary: once you have noticed the ubiquitous pattern with *à la, au, aux*, etc., you can understand at a glance phrases like:

>Ils sont partis à la pêche **à la** sardine.
>
>On va à la pêche **aux** crabes, demain?
>
>L'Écosse est un merveilleux endroit pour la pêche **au** saumon.

It's a good idea to get into the habit of recording in your dossier a word that interests you particularly. And when you do so, make a note of the patterns in which it occurs. You'll find that this helps you to remember vocabulary (and it improves your grammatical accuracy as well).

Activité 18

5   MINUTES

Look at the two photographs opposite and decide which word or phrase best completes the sentences below.

Regardez bien les deux photos ci-contre. Quelle expression complète chacune des descriptions?

1   Les pêcheurs d'alose ont l'air grave/joyeux

2   et ils sont habillés pour le travail/les vacances.

3   La photo de Batz-sur-Mer montre un groupe de copines/une famille

4   et les gens sont habillés pour le travail/les vacances.

Pêche à l'alose (*shad*) à Montjean-sur-Loire au début du vingtième siècle

Pêche aux crabes à Batz-sur-Mer, 1992

en passant » » » »

Il y a de plus en plus de pêcheurs amateurs en France. Trois millions de personnes pêchent au moins cinq jours par an. Si l'on compte les pêcheurs occasionnéls, le chiffre monte à cinq ou six millions. Cela représente un dixième de la population française. Et chose peu connue, cette proportion inclut au moins un quart de femmes!

» » » »

Linking ideas in writing

When you write a piece of continuous prose, however short, you have to ensure that there is a structure to the ideas, links between the individual sentences and a minimum of tiresome repetition. This is in sharp contrast to the style of, for example, a brochure, where most of the information is given without articles or verbs. To link your ideas, you need to use words like those in the table below.

Example	*Type of link created*
mais, au contraire	Refer to something that has already been said and introduce a contrasting idea or fact
en effet	Means 'indeed'; it explains and supplements a previous statement
elle, ils, etc.	Stand in for nouns or names already mentioned and help avoid repetition
soit … soit	Means 'either … or'; links alternatives
qui, que	Stand in for nouns or names already mentioned (more about these in Section 3)

These elements, whether they are single words or short phrases, are called link words. You will need them in any structured writing you have to do. You could list them in your dossier, building up your collection as you meet more and more of them.

Activité 19 asks you to work on structure and link words in a description of the two photographs on page 27. In this instance, the structure will be provided by a contrast (one paragraph about what went on then, one about what goes on now). The opposition is created by the use of *autrefois* and *aujourd'hui* and the correct choice of verb tense.

Activité 19
10 MINUTES

Put the phrases below in the correct order. The first and last phrases are already in the right place and the link words are in bold type. The punctuation also provides clues. There are two possible answers.

Réordonnez les expressions 2 à 8 pour former un texte cohérent. Les phrases 1 et 8 sont à la bonne place. Il y a deux réponses possibles.

1 Autrefois, la pêche était un passe-temps réservé aux hommes, et la majorité d'entre eux avait plus de trente ans.

2 **soit** à l'aube avant le travail,

3 **soit** les soirs d'été.

4 **En effet**, il ne faut pas oublier

5 **qui** partageaient silencieusement la même passion.

6 **Ils** se retrouvaient au bord de l'eau,

7 **que** 'le week-end' n'existait pas à cette époque.

8 C'étaient des pêcheurs sérieux,

9 Aujourd'hui, on va à la pêche en famille, avec femme et enfants, surtout pour profiter d'un après-midi au soleil.

As we have just seen, fishing for pleasure has changed over the years. It may be that things have also changed in an activity which interests you: perhaps you used to meet friends to do a sport and now you keep fit on your own; perhaps you used to cycle around your area but now the traffic makes this too dangerous; perhaps you used to go to the cinema with friends and now you watch videos with your family. In the next *activité* we want you to draw on your own experience to do a short piece of structured writing.

Activité 20
15 MINUTES

Write between forty and fifty words in French about an activity you do that has changed over the years. Try to re-use phrases which you have learned and some of the ones which we suggest below. The beginning of your story will require the use of the imperfect tense. If you are still not sure why, go back to the work you did on the imperfect in *Cadences*, Book 1. The answer in the *corrigé* follows the suggestions closely, but you should feel free to be more creative if you can!

Montrez comment l'un de vos loisirs a changé, dans une rédaction de cinquante mots maximum.

Suggestions for your writing

Start	autrefois, je…
Then say when	quand j'étais fatigué(e)
	quand j'étais en vacances
	quand j'étais étudiant(e)
	le soir, le dimanche, etc.
And with whom	soit … soit, e.g. soit avec un groupe de copines … soit en famille
Introduce a contrast	au contraire
	aujourd'hui, je…
And either say when and with whom	quand, avec, etc.
Or say why	parce que…
Or, if you want to supplement the information	en effet, je…

Finally, here is an *activité* designed to help you revise the structures and vocabulary which you have met in this section and some from Book 1 of *Cadences*. When you list pastimes, remember to use the correct forms of the article *du, de la, des* and when you talk about your friend imagine she's a woman and use the word you learned in *Activité 8*.

1 Listen to the audio extract and answer the questions according to the English prompts.

Écoutez l'extrait audio et répondez aux questions selon les indications en anglais.

2 Translate the following sentences into English, making them sound as natural as possible. The *corrigé* suggests some translations, but you may find others which are just as suitable (or even better).

Traduisez en anglais, le plus naturellement possible, les phrases suivantes.

(a) Si on va à Saint-Savinien, l'avantage c'est qu'on peut prendre une inscription pour des cours de tennis individuels.

(b) Quand je choisis une location, j'aime mieux une maison indépendante.

(c) J'ai commencé à pratiquer la voile quand j'avais de gros moyens financiers, et je continue parce que ça me passionne.

(d) Aux alentours du gîte, il y a de belles balades à faire à bicyclette.

(e) Autrefois, on pêchait entre hommes, surtout le dimanche à l'aube. Aujourd'hui, toute la famille peut apprécier un autre rythme de vie au bord de l'eau.

3 *Traduisez en français.*

(a) Gilbert used to do a lot of jogging before the accident.

(b) Every evening, we used to do body-building in the gym. (Use one of two ways of translating 'we'.)

(c) When you went away on holiday did you use to take a lot of books? (Use the imperfect tense and ask the question in two different ways.)

Now you've finished Section 1, it would be a good time to listen to the Feature Cassette, if you haven't done so already. It contains some of the language which you have learned in this section, but presents a very different hobby.

Faites le bilan

When you have finished this section of the book, you should be able to:

- Express when and how often you do certain leisure activities (*Activités 3, 4* and *20*).

- Justify a choice, orally and in writing (*Activité 7*).

- Recognize the 'filler' words *alors, bien sûr, eh bien* in a conversation (*Activité 11*).

- Receive oral directions and follow a route on a map (*Activité 9*).

- Recognize the link phrases *mais, par exemple, et puis, au contraire, en effet, soit ... soit* and use them appropriately in written French (*Activités 4, 19* and *20*).

- Recognize the difference between French with all syllables pronounced and French with dropped syllables (*Activités 13* and *14*).

Vocabulaire à retenir

1.1 *Que faites-vous de votre temps libre?*

faire du sport

faire de la voile

faire de la natation

faire du footing

faire de l'équitation

faire de la musculation

faire de la course

faire du badminton

avoir des loisirs

avoir du temps libre

régulièrement

tous les soirs/tous les vendredis

une fois par semaine/une fois par mois

de temps en temps

1.2 *Marcher pour le plaisir*

faire de la randonnée/de la marche (à pied)

une promenade

une détente

se détendre

partager

ça ne me dit rien

rester en forme

un gymnase

1.3 *S'échapper des villes*

un sportif, une sportive

faire de la gymnastique

une salle de sport

en salle

quand je peux m'échapper

une balade

une montée

une descente

un panorama

ça en vaut la peine

1.4 Vos loisirs dans notre région

un gîte

un coin calme/un joli coin

un propriétaire, une propriétaire

sur place

la voiture est indispensable

il n'y a pas grand-chose à faire

quand même

les alentours de Vallonne/Nantes

aux alentours de Vallonne/Nantes

à partir de

la location

prendre une inscription

l'hébergement

un cours particulier/collectif

aimer mieux

un pêcheur

se retrouver le dimanche/le soir

2 Les loisirs chez soi

STUDY CHART

	Topic	Activity/timing	Audio/video	Key points
30 mins	2.1 La collection	22 (15 mins)	Video	Watching and understanding a video portrait
1 hr	2.2 Ne laissez pas passer l'occasion	23 (15 mins)		Recognizing the direct object pronoun *le, la, les*
		24 (10 mins)		Using the direct object pronoun *le, la, les* in writing
		25 (25 mins)	Audio	Using the direct object pronoun *le, la, les* orally
1 hr 10 mins	2.3 Le plaisir de cuisiner	26 (10 mins)		Vocabulary: cooking
		27 (15 mins)		Using verbs in the imperative
		28 (15 mins)		Background to the *pieds-noirs*
		29 (10 mins)	Video	Watching a recipe being made
1 hr 20 mins	2.4 Les loisirs à domicile. les temps changent	30 (10 mins)		Writing about changing trends in leisure patterns
		31 (15 mins)		Vocabulary: home leisure pursuits
		32 (15 mins)		Talking about your own home leisure pursuits
		33 (30 mins)	Audio	Section revision

*I*n the previous section we looked at leisure activities in general. Here, we're going to concentrate on hobbies people do at home (*chez soi*, literally 'at one's home'). We begin in *La collection* with Philippe, a business studies student, whose main hobby is collecting. Collections are often built up by buying, selling and swapping items through newspaper adverts. You will see how this is done and also some of the surprising things that become collectable. To some, cooking is a chore; to others, it is a hobby. In *Le plaisir de cuisiner* (the joy of cooking) you will learn to read recipes in French and see one of them prepared by Henri, an enthusiastic cook, in his own kitchen. The final topic in this section, *Les loisirs à domicile*, presents data about changing trends in home leisure activities in France.

In this section you'll work on the subjects and objects of verbs and learn about the form of verbs used to give instructions.

2.1 La collection

In the first topic you will see a video portrait of Philippe, who derives great pleasure from his relationship with cars, but perhaps in ways you might not expect. Your main aim in watching the video is to gain insights into Philippe's world, culture and personality, although the topic also gives you an opportunity to revise regular and irregular past participles and to learn some conversational phrases.

As he drives home and then settles down to an interview in his room, Philippe talks about two topics which are central to his life and well-being, and a third which is to do with his father. Watch out for these changes in the settings and topics of the interview when you play the video.

Activité 22
15 MINUTES
VIDEO

1 Watch the *La collection* video sequence straight through (20:48–25:10) and identify the three main topics Philippe talks about.

Regardez la séquence vidéo en entier et cherchez à reconnaître les trois thèmes principaux.

Pour vous aider

j'aime beaucoup conduire I love driving

ça a complètement changé ma vie it has radically changed my life

cela m'a donné beaucoup de liberté it's given me enormous freedom

elle a été aménagée it has been adapted

pour moi, exprès specifically for me (the more usual word order is *exprès pour moi*) *ça dépend*   it depends

des fois … d'autres fois   sometimes … at other times (*des fois* is used in spoken or relaxed French only)

2   In his specially adapted car Philippe says that three things make it possible for him to drive. Below is a transcript of what he says. Translate the words in bold type into English.

Traduisez les expressions en gras.

> **… quand j'ai eu ma voiture, ça a complètement changé ma vie, cela m'a donné beaucoup de liberté.**
>
> **J'ai eu ma voiture il y a trois ans. Elle a été aménagée pour moi, exprès**, c'est-à-dire qu'on a fait mettre à Paris des commandes spéciales qui me sont adaptées: j'ai, par exemple, un volant plus petit ou alors un accélérateur plus près de moi.

3   Two of the past participles which you translated are irregular. Write out the infinitive form for each, after revising the formation of the perfect tense in *Cadences*, Book 1, if necessary.

Écrivez les deux infinitifs correspondant aux participes passés que vous avez traduits.

Stressing a fact

Did you notice the amazement in the interviewer's voice when he remarked on Philippe's father's collection:

> Vous avez un nombre phénoménal de bandes dessinées!… Il faut le dire.

Il faut le dire can be translated as 'it has to be said'. In this case the interviewer's amazement could be shown by translating the sentence as:

> You have a tremendous collection of cartoons, I must say!

You can also use *il faut le dire* to stress other facts or ideas. For example:

> *La plage est un peu sale, il faut le dire!*
> It has to be admitted that the beach is rather dirty!
>
> *Le défilé était très bien organisé, il faut le dire!*
> The procession was very well organized, it has to be said!

It might be a good idea to create a new heading in your dossier, 'How to stress a point'. Put *il faut le dire* in there and add other ways of emphasizing things as you come across them. Practise saying them in your head (or aloud) several times over the next week, so as to memorize them.

2.2 *Ne laissez pas passer l'occasion!*

Saisissez l'occasion à la foire à la brocante!

We now enter a world of bargains, second-hand buying, selling and swapping, junk (*la brocante*) and antique dealers (*les antiquaires*). *Laisser passer l'occasion* means 'to miss the chance' or 'to miss the opportunity'. (You may remember this meaning of *occasion* from *c'est l'occasion de retrouver le vrai goût des choses* in the text *Marcher pour le plaisir*.) The title of this topic also puns on two other meanings of *une occasion*, a second-hand object and a bargain. For example:

> *Ma voiture est une occasion/j'ai une voiture d'occasion.*
> My car is second hand.

'Ma voiture est une occasion!'

> *Cet appartement, c'est une occasion!*
> That flat is a real bargain!

You may remember Philippe being asked how collectors operated. Did they buy models? Swap them? He answered:

> Ça dépend! Des fois, on les achète dans les magasins et d'autres fois, on se les échange ou on se les achète entre collectionneurs.

One way of buying or swapping is to consult the small ads (*faire les petites annonces*) to search for interesting objects and curios. One of the features of small ads is their conciseness. In particular, little words like *le, la, les* are often omitted. This makes an ads page an ideal starting-point for work on these forms.

Small ads also contain useful phrases to describe prices: people will give a good price (*acheter cher*) or claim to sell at a cheap price (*vendre bon marché*). Note that *cher* and *bon marché* do not change when used with a feminine or a plural noun. Thus, *j'ai acheté la Bugatti cher* or *je vends les petites voitures bon marché*. Finally, the phrase *ça vaut très cher* (plural *ils/elles valent très cher*) is also worth remembering, as it means 'it's/they're worth a lot of money'.

In small ads people usually say, in the first-person singular, that they are looking for items (*cherche, recherche*) or that they want to do certain types of transaction: *achète, vends, offre* and *échange*.

In the next *activité* you will be concentrating on *le, la* and *les* forms in preparation for learning about pronouns.

Activité 23
15 MINUTES

1   Read *Les petites annonces* (overleaf), concentrating on what kinds of transaction are taking place. It is less important to understand all the vocabulary, so try not to use your dictionary.

Lisez les petites annonces qui se trouvent à la page suivante et cherchez à comprendre les transactions désirées par les auteurs.

2   Here are summaries of some of the ads, but crucial information has been left out. To identify the goods on offer, find the noun which stands for each of the words in bold. Write it down and then say whether it is masculine or feminine, singular or plural.

Remplacez chacun des mots en gras par le nom correspondant et dites s'il est masculin ou féminin, singulier ou pluriel.

(a) Il **les** offre gracieusement.

(b) Il **les** achète en bon état et il accepte toutes les marques.

(c) Ils **l'**achètent ou **l'**échangent contre des timbres poste.

3 The collectors who wrote these ads are discussing deals. Name the object which you think each person in the following sentences is asking about, giving the appropriate definite article *le*, *la* or *les* with it.

De quoi parlent ces collectionneurs?

(a) Je le cherche parce que j'ai déjà le reste de la série.

(b) Ah, je la vends bon marché. 60 000 francs, c'est pas cher!

(c) Oui, je la vends aussi, mais avec des lits jumeaux 1920.

(d) Vous me garantissez qu'elles sont anciennes et en très bon état? Alors d'accord, je les achète cher.

PETITES ANNONCES PETITES ANNONCES

• Achète appareils-photos en bon état toutes marques : Krauss, Photosphère, Zeiss, Leïca. Tél.: 4 62 53 14

• Antiquaires achètent collection de modèles réduits ou échangent contre timbres poste. Tél.: 7 64 17 50

• Occasion. Vends lits jumeaux 1920 et cheminée marbre style Louis XV. Cartes état-major toilées 1880–1910. Cherche volume 1 de la série *Monseigneur Le Vin*. Tél.: 7 52 1750

• Achète cher machines à coudre 1875, machines à écrire et à calculer anciennes. Tél.: 3 12 22 47

• Recherche cartes postales anciennes des départements français, en très bon état. Achat ou échange si la qualité est satisfaisante. Tél.: 4 11 40 50

• Offre gracieusement livres et vieux documents navigation sur la Loire. Tél.: 3 15 67 47

• Vends bon marché bibliothèque 1200 livres psychanalyse-sociologie à l'état neuf, 60 000 F. Tél.: 4 23 23 12

Pour vous aider

appareils-photos cameras (for stills)

antiquaires antique dealers (thus *chez un antiquaire* means 'in an antique shop')

modèles réduits model cars

achat purchase

gracieusement free (used in advertising language; the other meaning of *gracieusement* is 'graciously')

bibliothèque book collection

Recognizing subjects and objects

When learning a foreign language it's important to know what we mean by the grammatical terms 'subject' and 'object'. The subject is the person or thing performing the action of the verb and the object is the person or thing on which the action is carried out. If, in a particular case, you have difficulty deciding what the subject or object of the verb is, the following technique should help you.

Start by identifying the verb. Ask yourself who or what is performing the action of the verb. This will tell you who or what the subject is. Next, ask yourself who or what the verb affects. This will tell you who or what the object of the verb is. Take the sentence:

> Véronique achète une maison.

The verb is *achète*. The person who is doing the buying is Véronique, so the word 'Véronique' is the subject. The thing that is being bought is the house, so *maison* is the object.

We're now going to look at words which are the objects of verbs. In particular, you will learn how to use object pronouns.

The object pronouns 'le', 'la', 'les'

As we saw, ad writers use few words, choosing them for description and information. In continuous prose or normal conversation, however, you also need words like *le, la, les* and they must be in the right position and in the correct form. In particular, you need pronouns, which can be substituted for a previously mentioned noun, thus allowing you to avoid repetition. Here we are going to concentrate on the form and position of those pronouns that stand in for the object of a verb.

The object pronouns *le, la* and *les* look exactly the same as the definite article. Here is an example of the object pronoun in the feminine singular form. It is shown in bold type.

- — Tu vois la voiture rouge?
- — Non, quelle voiture rouge?
- — Là, devant le restaurant.
- — Ah oui, je **la** vois!

English distinguishes between people (him, her, them) and things (it, them) in its use of object pronouns. Gender is taken into account for people only. In French the same pronouns serve for people and things, but, in the singular, the object pronouns *le* and *la* always reflect gender, see *la* and *voiture* in the example above. The singular form *l'* and the plural form *les* do not themselves show gender.

The examples below illustrate how pronoun forms show gender and number.

> Je vois un **camion** là-bas, tu **le** vois?
>
> Il répare des vieilles **voitures** et il **les** revend.
>
> On collectionne des petits **camions** et on **les** échange.
>
> J'adore ma **sœur**, mais malheureusement je **la** vois rarement.

Here are two examples of the singular form *l'*.

> Je vends mon **camion**. Tu **l'**achètes?
>
> J'ai vu une petite **voiture** de collection qui me plaisait et je **l'**ai achetée.

Notice the position of the object pronoun: it comes before the verb, or before the first part of the verb if you are using a form of verb that has two parts, like the perfect tense.

The examples above show *le, la* and *les* standing in for particular things or people. However, the object pronoun can also stand in for a general idea. For example, towards the end of the video sequence featuring Philippe, the interviewer says '*il faut le dire*'. The *le* here stands for the whole of the interviewer's previous remark: '*Vous avez un nombre phénoménal de bandes dessinées!*' When it stands for a general idea, the pronoun is always masculine singular.

The pronouns you have just studied are called direct object pronouns. The reason for this name is given in the Study Guide glossary under 'Object'. You may want to consult this glossary entry now, or at some later time. The important thing for the moment is that, from now on, you should make sure that you use these pronouns correctly. If you have time, make a note of them in your dossier whenever you use them in the rest of this book, particularly if you discover in a *corrigé* that you have used them incorrectly.

At this stage, we don't expect you to know about the agreement of direct object pronouns and past participles, but reading pages 147–8, paragraph (ii), in your Grammar Book will give you the basic rules if you wish to go a little bit further.

To practise forming and positioning direct object pronouns, do the following two *activités*.

Activité 24
10 MINUTES

1 Read the ads (a)–(e) opposite. Look at the words set in bold type and decide whether they are masculine, feminine, singular or plural.

Lisez les annonces (a)–(e) ci-contre. Examinez les mots en gras et notez s'ils sont 'masculin', 'féminin', 'singulier' ou 'pluriel'.

(a) Vends pour cause changement d'adresse **bibliothèque** 1 200 volumes.

(b) Vends **album** de photos signées, occasion unique.

(c) Vends **lits** jumeaux. Contactez le 03 96 22.

(d) Vends **machines** à coudre 1875.

(e) Vends ou échange **magazine** satirique édition 1939.

2   You want to buy all these things, if the price is right. For each of the ads, write out a question asking for the price of the object(s). We have done the first one for you.

Rédigez une phrase pour demander le prix de chaque objet en imitant le modèle ci-dessous.

La bibliothèque, vous la vendez combien?

3   You're happy to buy at the price quoted. For each of the ads below, write out what you would say to the seller. Don't forget to change *vendre* to *acheter* in the present tense and to use the correct pronoun.

Complétez les phrases suivantes avec le verbe 'acheter' au présent. N'oubliez pas d'utiliser le pronom qui convient.

(a) D'accord, la bibliothèque, je _____ _____ .

(b) Dans ce cas, l'album de photos, je _____ _____ .

(c) Eh bien oui, les lits jumeaux, je _____ _____ .

(d) Elles sont bon marché, les machines à coudre: je _____ _____ .

In the next *activité* you are asked to talk about treasured possessions, both other people's and your own. Perhaps it's an antique which is worth quite a bit; on the other hand, it could be a curio that you picked up for next to nothing or that has great sentimental value for you (*ça a une grande valeur sentimentale pour vous*). First, you have to reply to some questions according to prompts on the tape. You'll need to remember how to use *bon marché* and *ça vaut/ils valent très cher*. Then we ask you a few personal questions and you can talk about favourite objects of your own. You should do this out loud or record yourself.

Activité 25

25 MINUTES

AUDIO 11

117.

1   Read the sentences (a) to (d) below and make a mental note of whether the words in bold are masculine or feminine, singular or plural. Then write the corresponding direct object pronoun after each sentence. We've done the first one for you.

Lisez les phrases. Après chacune, écrivez le pronom qui correspond au mot en gras.

(a) Tu as un nombre phénoménal de **bandes** dessinées! (les)

(b) Tu as trouvé les **cartes** postales où?

(c) Il paraît que tu vends tes **modèles** réduits?

(d) Tu vends aussi cette **Citroën** miniature?

2   You are now going to use similar though not identical phrases to take part in a conversation in which somebody is showing their room to a friend. Cover up your answers to step 1. Play Audio Extract 11 and answer the five questions on the tape, making sure that you use the correct pronouns. English prompts will help you decide what to say.

Écoutez l'extrait et répondez aux questions en français selon les indications données en anglais.

3   Think about something you bought which now has great sentimental value for you. Name it in (a) below, then complete sentences (b) to (d). Use direct object pronouns, remembering to adapt each pronoun according to whether the possession you have in mind is a masculine or a feminine noun in French. In (a) you will also have to delete the article which does not show the correct agreement, and in (b) and (c) the incorrect past participles.

Complétez les phrases ci-dessous.

(a) J'ai un ___chien___ /une _____
    qui a une grande valeur sentimentale pour moi.

(b) Je ___l'___ ai trouvé/trouvée ___chez un éleveur de chien___. (say where)

(c) Je ___l'___ ai acheté/achetée ___cher___. (say whether cheap or expensive)

(d) Either
    (i) J'ai l'intention de ___le___ garder toujours.
    or
    (ii) J'ai quand même l'intention de _____ vendre un jour si j'ai besoin d'argent.

2.3 Le plaisir de cuisiner

In this topic we focus on cooking for pleasure at home. You'll begin by finding out how to read a recipe (and also how to cook it) and then watch a keen amateur cook as he prepares a dinner for his friends.

Apart from cooking vocabulary, which always comes in handy when talking to French people, you'll learn how to give and receive instructions.

Les bonnes recettes

The first recipe you're going to work on is for *Veau jardinière. Jardinière* (or *à la jardinière)* is a name given to recipes involving small spring vegetables, ideally grown in the garden.

The next *activité* begins with a simple vocabulary exercise. You'll then use link words to help you rearrange the paragraphs of the jumbled-up recipe. To do this *activité*, you need to know the cooking expression *faire revenir*, which means 'to turn in hot oil or fat until pale gold' and applies to all sorts of food. For example: *faites revenir les oignons* (fry the onions until they change colour); *quand les morceaux de poulet sont bien revenus* (when the chicken pieces are golden). This is a rather strange use of *revenir*. It's other meaning is 'to come back' or 'to return' and is totally unconnected with the idea of frying! When talking about cooking, *revenir* is often used with *faire* or with *être*, as in the examples above.

Faites revenir les oignons!

1 Here are the start and the end of the recipe for *Veau jardinière* – the ingredients and the final recommendations to the cook. Read them, checking words in the dictionary if necessary.

Lisez le début et la fin de la recette, et vérifiez que vous connaissez le vocabulaire.

Veau jardinière
Ingrédients pour 6 personnes

1,5 kg de veau

2 kg de petits pois frais

500 g d'oignons blancs

500 g de carottes

4 petits navets

du persil

du beurre

du sel

du poivre

une feuille de laurier

2 morceaux de sucre

de l'huile

2 litres d'eau pour le bouillon

un grand récipient

Choisissez du veau de seconde qualité. Il est beaucoup moins cher que l'escalope, mais pour faire à la jardinière, il est tout aussi délicieux.

Servez bien chaud.

Si vous souhaitez adopter une variante rapide, faites cuire 15 minutes dans l'autocuiseur. Ce plat est exquis à la saison des petits pois frais, et on l'apprécie également réchauffé. Accompagnez-le d'une salade de cœurs de laitue.

2 Read the five captions (a)–(e) opposite, which describe the main steps in the recipe. Underline six expressions which show at what point certain things are to be done. All the expressions are at the start of sentences.

Lisez les cinq descriptions ci-dessous. Soulignez six expressions qui montrent l'ordre de la préparation du Veau jardinière. Ces expressions sont toutes en début de phrase.

(a) Pendant ce temps, épluchez les carottes et les navets. Écossez les petits pois frais. Coupez tous les légumes en petits morceaux, mais laissez les oignons entiers.

(b) Puis mélangez les légumes et ajoutez-les au bouillon, avec deux morceaux de sucre. Remettez le couvercle. Finissez la cuisson à feu très doux.

(c) Ensuite, couvrez avec de l'eau bouillante. Mettez sur feu doux. Laissez cuire, avec un couvercle, environ une heure et demie.

(d) Quand le veau est presque prêt, enlevez le persil et rajoutez un petit peu de beurre.

(e) D'abord, coupez la viande en morceaux. Faites-la revenir dans un peu d'huile. Une fois qu'elle est dorée, mettez-la dans un grand récipient avec un peu de sel, de poivre, une feuille de laurier et un bouquet de persil.

3   Now look at the five pictures below, which show the main stages of the recipe in the correct order. Which caption belongs with which picture?

Associez chaque description à une des illustrations ci-dessous.

1

2

3

4

5

Using the imperative to give instructions

In the veal recipe did you notice the verb forms used to give instructions? For instance:

> **Coupez** la viande en morceaux.
>
> **Choisissez** du veau.

They are in the imperative, which is used to give instructions or commands. You are already familiar with this form from reading our instructions in this course, where we frequently tell you: *écoutez, enregistrez, écrivez, trouvez,* etc.

You may have noticed the hyphen after some of the imperative verbs.

> Puis mélangez les légumes et **ajoutez-les** au bouillon.
>
> Une fois qu'elle est dorée, **mettez-la** dans un grand récipient.

When you use an imperative, the direct object pronoun comes **after** the verb (not before it as you saw earlier in this section when studying pronouns). You may have already noted examples of this structure, as it occurs frequently in our French instructions: *notez-les, écoutez-la,* etc. If you are writing, remember to link the verb and the object pronoun with a hyphen, as in the examples above.

You will find advice on how to form the imperative in your Grammar Book, pages 133–4, paragraphs (a) and (b), but it will help you if you also make a note in your dossier of a few imperatives to use in common situations and try to memorize them. Choose some which you might need for practical purposes. For example:

> **Faites** attention! (for warning a pedestrian not to step into the road)
>
> **Fais** attention! (same situation, to a child)
>
> **Prenez** à droite/à gauche (giving a stranger directions)
>
> **Prends** à droite/à gauche (giving a friend directions)
>
> **Entrez**! (to a visitor on formal terms) and **Entre**! (to a friend or a child visitor)

In shops you can ask for things to be done for you by adding *-moi* after the imperative:

> **Donnez-moi** du/de la/des (whatever it is), s'il vous plaît.
>
> **Faites-moi** un paquet-cadeau, s'il vous plaît.

Although this may sound rather abrupt in comparison with polite English forms such as 'Would you mind wrapping this up for me please', it is perfectly acceptable to a French shopkeeper – providing it is followed by *s'il vous plaît* of course!

The next *activité* will help you practise the main grammar points studied in this section, by asking you to use imperatives and direct object pronouns together.

Activité 27
15 MINUTES

You are teaching a good friend how to make *Veau jardinière* from the recipe which you studied earlier. Answer his questions (in the *tu* form), filling the gaps with verbs in the imperative present and with direct object pronouns, as appropriate.

Remplissez les trous pour expliquer la recette du Veau jardinière. Utilisez des impératifs au présent et des pronoms objets directs.

Question   Bon, j'ai la viande, je commence par faire quoi?

Réponse   D'abord, _____ - _____ en morceaux.

Question   Et après?

Réponse   _____ - _____ _____ dans
            un peu d'huile.

Question   Et quand elle est revenue?

Réponse   Une fois qu'elle est dorée, _____ - _____
            dans un grand récipient.

Question   Combien de temps je la laisse cuire?

Réponse   _____ - _____ _____ , avec
            un couvercle, environ une heure et demie.

Question   Et qu'est-ce que je fais pendant qu'elle cuit?

Réponse   Pendant ce temps, _____ les carottes et les
            navets. _____ les petits pois frais.

Question   Qu'est-ce que je fais de tous ces légumes?

Réponse   _____ - _____ en petits morceaux, mais
            _____ les oignons entiers.

Question   Et puis?

Réponse   Puis _____ les légumes et
            _____ - _____ au bouillon, avec deux
            morceaux de sucre. _____ le couvercle.
            _____ la cuisson à feu très doux.

Henri fait la cuisine

In the video sequence which you're going to watch next, Henri has invited some friends to dinner and is getting the meal ready, working from his book of *Cuisine pied-noir* recipes. First, though, here is a short text about the *pieds-noirs* and their cooking traditions.

Activité 28

15 MINUTES

1   *Lisez le texte suivant.*

Les pieds-noirs

Dans les années soixante, 100 000 personnes sont arrivées en France, rapatriées d'Algérie. On appelait ces Français, établis en Algérie pendant la colonisation du XIXème siècle, les 'pieds-noirs'. On a proposé de nombreuses explications à ce surnom: par exemple, certains disent qu'il est dû aux bottes noires qu'ils portaient. D'autres pensent que l'expression vient du fait que les pieds-noirs étaient nés sur le sol africain. Ce nom est resté après l'indépendance de l'Algérie en 1962, et continue à être utilisé. Il existe, bien sûr, une culture pied-noir et une cuisine pied-noir, influencées par les traditions de l'Afrique du Nord. Le signe le plus visible de la culture pied-noir, c'est l'arrivée en France de plats comme le couscous, avec sa sauce piquante, ou les saucisses épicées appelées 'merguez'. Beaucoup de restaurants spécialisés dans le couscous ont ouvert leurs portes pour présenter aux Français une cuisine exotique, aux saveurs fortes, et peu chère. Les restaurants de couscous ont connu un grand succès, et aujourd'hui ce plat est devenu le symbole de la relation entre les trois cultures: française, nord-africaine et pied-noir.

Pour vous aider

il est dû aux bottes noires qu'ils portaient   it comes from the black boots they used to wear

épicées   spicy or hot

ont connu un grand succès   have been very successful

2   *Expliquez en anglais qui sont les pieds-noirs.*

3   What is the *faux-ami* (see Study Guide glossary) in the third sentence? What does it mean in English?

   Trouvez le faux-ami de la troisième phrase et donnez sa traduction en anglais.

4   Does this development in the range of a nation's cuisine have any parallels in Great Britain?

Y a-t-il en Grande-Bretagne des exemples similaires dans l'évolution des spécialités culinaires?

5   Underline the past participles in the text.

Soulignez les participes passés du texte.

Henri comes from a *pied-noir* family himself, hence his choice of menu for a dinner. As he explains, he's having some friends round (*je reçois des amis*) and so he and his wife thought they'd cook them a couscous (*et donc on a décidé de leur faire un couscous*). Possibly his friends asked him to make a couscous, knowing Henri's skill with North African cuisine. In France, when invited by close friends to a meal, it isn't considered impolite to request a favourite dish. You could use your knowledge of the imperative and answer an invitation to dinner for next Saturday like this:

> *Samedi prochain? Oh oui, et fais-moi une tarte aux fraises!*

Activité 29
10 MINUTES
V I D E O

1   Now watch the video sequence *Henri fait la cuisine* (25:12–30:29). Many of the cooking processes which Henri demonstrates will be familiar to you from the *Veau jardinière* recipe, although obviously the ingredients are different. As you watch, listen in particular for what Henri says about traditions.

Regardez Henri préparer son couscous et écoutez particulièrement ce qu'il dit des traditions.

Pour vous aider

il s'agit d'un mélange   what we have here is a mixture (*il s'agit de* is a very common phrase, used to introduce a topic; can be translated as 'here we have', 'what we are talking about is' or 'it is', according to context)

des quatre épices   allspice (literally four spices)

des fèves   broad beans

des pois chiches   chick peas

des cœurs d'artichauts   artichoke hearts

le faitout   the cooking pot (literally for doing 'everything' in)

mettre la semoule à gonfler   to leave the semolina to swell

à la vapeur   in steam

la veille   the day before

2   *Répondez en anglais aux questions suivantes.*

   (a) According to Henri, when is this dish served in Algeria?

   (b) What is the difference in cooking time between the traditional and the rapid methods of making couscous?

3   To review your work on direct object pronouns, go over the transcript of *Henri fait la cuisine* in your Transcript Booklet, underlining these

pronouns and being particularly careful to notice the difference between them and the definite articles.

Dans la transcription de 'Henri fait la cuisine', soulignez les pronoms objets directs.

Although Henri didn't mention it, a couscous is best enjoyed with the very hot 'harissa' sauce normally served with it!

en passant » » » »

In France, when you are asked to a meal at someone's house, the done thing is to take flowers or a really nice cake or dessert bought in a pâtisserie, or some exotic treat. Don't take wine: your host will already have chosen a suitable wine to go with the meal.   » » » »

2.4 Les loisirs à domicile: les temps changent

In this topic we look at recent shifts in the leisure patterns of French people when they're at home (*à domicile*). The diagram opposite shows changes recorded between 1967 and 1988 by the INSEE, the Institut National de la Statistique et des Études Économiques, the main collector of sociological data in France. This information is interesting in itself, but you are also going to use it to revise how to form the perfect tense and to learn some more ways to say how often something happens.

Activité 30
10 MINUTES

1   Using the data from the diagram, complete the following sentences. Use the perfect tense (check its formation in Book 1 of *Cadences*, Section 2, if necessary).

Les chiffres suivants représentent le pourcentage de Français qui ont fait quoi, en 1988? Avec l'information donnée dans le schéma, complétez les phrases suivantes.

Exemple
Pendant l'année 1988 82% des Français ont regardé la télévision tous les jours ou presque.

(a) Pendant l'année 1988 75% des Français ont…

(b) Pendant l'année 1988 7% des Français ont…

(c) Pendant l'année 1988 31% des Français ont…

(d) Pendant l'année 1988 64% des Français ont…

Proportion de Français ayant pratiqué l'activité suivante en 1967 et en 1988

| 1967 |
| 1988 |

Regarder la télévision tous les jours ou presque

51%
82%

Jouer de la musique régulièrement ou parfois

4%
7%

Recevoir des parents ou des amis pour un repas au moins une fois par mois

39%
64%

Réparer une voiture de temps en temps et 'avec plaisir'

10%
12%

Lire une revue ou un magazine régulièrement

56%
79%

Lire au moins un livre par mois

32%
31%

Écouter la radio tous les jours ou presque

67%
75%

Jardiner tous les jours ou presque à la belle saison

20%
19%

Jouer aux cartes chaque semaine ou presque

13%
18%

Lire un quotidien tous les jours ou presque

60%
42%

Source: based on data in Mermet, 1990, p. 357

Pour vous aider

à la belle saison   in the summer   *un quotidien*   a daily newspaper

2   Complete the following sentences to show whether the number of people involved in a particular activity has gone up or down. Use the perfect tense and the verbs *augmenter* and *diminuer*.

Comment le nombre de personnes qui pratiquent les activités suivantes a-t-il changé entre 1967 et 1988?

(a)   Le nombre de gens qui reçoivent des parents ou des amis pour un repas au moins une fois par mois a _____ .

(b)   La proportion des lecteurs de quotidiens a _____ .

(c)   Le nombre des téléspectateurs a _____ .

(d)   Le pourcentage de gens qui pratiquent le jardinage a _____ .

The next *activité* gives you an overview of what are currently the most common home leisure activities in France. You should learn all the leisure vocabulary in it.

1   Use the information in the diagram on the previous page to fill in the phrases missing from the text below, putting the verbs in the perfect tense.

Remplissez les trous et mettez les verbes au passé composé.

Au cours de l'année 1988, on constate que 82% des Français

_____ la télévision tous les jours ou presque, contre 42% qui

_____ un quotidien et 75% qui _____ la

radio. De plus, 64 % _____ des parents ou des amis pour un

repas au moins une fois par mois. 79% _____ une revue ou

un magazine régulièrement et 31% un livre au moins une fois par mois.

Enfin, 12% _____ une voiture avec plaisir. Pour l'année

1988, on n'a pas de statistiques sur la proportion de gens qui regardent

régulièrement des vidéos au magnétoscope. D'une manière générale, on

peut dire que les Français pratiquent beaucoup de loisirs à domicile, et

notamment des loisirs culturels.

2   *Traduisez les deux dernières phrases en anglais.*

What about you? How much time have you spent on leisure activities at home over the last twelve months? Now is your chance to say what is true for you. Use as many expressions of time as you can.

Decide which of the pastimes in the diagram on page 51 apply to you. Then say out loud or record a description of your activities, starting *Au cours de l'année dernière, j'ai...* . Change the expressions of time to suit your circumstances. For example, you could vary the period described (*toutes les semaines, tous les quinze jours, toutes les quinzaines, tous les mois*) or the number of times (*plus d'une fois par..., deux or trois fois par..., de temps en temps*). You could say that you did your activity *le plus souvent possible*, or perhaps only *une fois ou deux dans l'année*.

Notez ce que vous avez fait pendant votre temps libre au cours de l'année dernière et expliquez-le à voix haute ou enregistrez-vous.

If you would like to revise the work you did on dates, numbers and percentages in Book 1 of *Cadences*, you could try reading out loud the information given here *en passant*.

en passant » » » »

Voici quelques tendances en matière de vidéo: en 1990, 66% des Britanniques avaient un magnétoscope, contre 31% des Français. En France, les gens qui ont un magnétoscope possèdent en moyenne vingt-huit cassettes vidéo. 58% des utilisateurs louent des cassettes préenregistrées et 30% préfèrent en acheter. La location de magnétoscopes intéresse 40% de familles en Grande-Bretagne, contre 1% seulement en France! (Chiffres provenant de Mermet, 1990)

Proportion de la population ayant un magnétoscope		Location de magnétoscopes (par famille)	
1990		**1990**	
France	31%	France	1%
Grande-Bretagne	66%	Grande-Bretagne	40%

» » » »

Finally, here is a revision *activité* in two parts: first a speaking exercise, then a translation to help you check that you have remembered the vocabulary and grammar from this section.

Activité 33

30 MINUTES

AUDIO 12

' 5 0

1   Listen to the audio extract and answer the questions in the gaps, as prompted.

Écoutez l'extrait et répondez de la manière indiquée.

2   *Traduisez les phrases suivantes en français.*

(a) 42% of French people read a newspaper every day.

(b) I cook for pleasure. I like to entertain relatives or friends for a meal.

(c) The French in Algeria (*d'Algérie*) were given the nickname *pieds-noirs*.

(d) Be careful, an antique chair like this is worth a lot! (Use the *vous* form.)

(e) We had some friends round last month. (Use the perfect tense.)

(f) Buy the books, they're selling them cheap. (Use the *tu* form.)

(g) It has completely changed my life, I have to say!

Faites le bilan

When you have finished this section of the book, you should be able to:

- Use direct object pronouns correctly to refer to people and things, in written and spoken French (*Activités 24, 25* and *27*).

- Understand and use the imperative in spoken and written French, in the *tu* and the *vous* forms (*Activités 27* and *33*).

- Recognize and use the phrases of time *tous les jours ou presque, chaque semaine ou presque, une fois par...* (*Activités 30* and *32*).

- Recognize the adverbs and phrases of time *puis, ensuite, d'abord, une fois que, pendant ce temps* (*Activités 26* and *27*).

Vocabulaire à retenir

2.1 La collection

chez soi

ça a complètement changé ma vie

ça m'a donné beaucoup de liberté

aménagé, e

exprès pour moi/pour lui

comment vous faites?

ça dépend

2.2 Ne laissez pas passer l'occasion

laisser passer une occasion

faire les petites annonces

une voiture d'occasion

en bon état

échanger

acheter/vendre quelque chose cher

acheter/vendre quelque chose bon marché

cela vaut très cher/ils valent très cher

c'est bon marché/ils sont bon marché

2.3 Le plaisir de cuisiner

ensuite

d'abord

une fois que la viande est dorée/ une fois que les amis sont arrivés

environ une heure et demie

faire cuire des légumes/de la viande

mélanger

épicé, e

un pied-noir, une pied-noir

recevoir des amis

il s'agit d'un mélange de viande/ d'une occasion merveilleuse

ajouter de l'eau/du sucre

la veille

2.4 Les loisirs à domicile: les temps changent

à domicile

jardiner

un quotidien

un magnétoscope

augmenter

diminuer

3 Le travail au quotidien

STUDY CHART

	Topic	Activity/timing	Audio/video	Key points
2 hrs 30 mins	3.1 Les horaires	34 (20 mins)	Video	Recognizing expressions describing work routines
		35 (10 mins)	Audio	Describing work routines orally
		36 (20 mins)	Video	Vocabulary: work routines
		37 (15 mins)		Giving a short talk
		38 (15 mins)		
		39 (15 mins)	Audio	Recognizing phrases for working hours
		40 (20 mins)		Trends in French working hours
2 hrs 30mins	3.2 C'est un beau métier?	41 (20 mins)	Audio	Recognizing phrases describing advantages and disadvantages
		42 (15 mins)	Audio	Stating advantages and disadvantages
		43 (15 mins)	Audio	Summarizing a short audio extract in English
		44 (15 mins)	Audio	Listening to someone describing a job and understanding in detail
		45 (15 mins)		Introduction of *qui* and *que*
		46 (30 mins)		Practising the use of *qui* and *que*
		47 (15 mins)		Reading about health hazards at work
2 hrs	3.3 Les femmes et le travail	48 (30 mins)	Video	Vocabulary: domestic timetable and household tasks
		49 (10 mins)	Audio	Talking about entitlements and conditions at work
		50 (30 mins)		Writing about domestic duties
		51 (5 mins)	Audio	Recognizing and practising the sound [j]
		52 (25 mins)		Section revision

*I*n this section a number of people describe their day-to-day working lives (*au quotidien* means on a day-to-day basis). In *Les horaires* we look at the different routines people follow and at the trends for working hours in France as a whole. Then, in *C'est un beau métier?*, we hear people talking about the advantages and disadvantages of their work Finally, in *Les femmes et le travail,* we look at the problems of combining work with family responsibilities.

As you work on these topics, you will learn how to describe your own routines, extend your vocabulary and learn a new point of grammar which will help you structure sentences in French.

3.1 Les horaires

The video and audio recordings in this topic feature Véronique (*la boulangère*), Colette (*l'éclusière*) and Alain, a fire-fighter (*un pompier*), talking about the rhythms of their working lives. The yearly work pattern of a wine grower (*un viticulteur*) is explained to us by Claude Papin. We end with a text which looks at recent trends in French working hours.

Véronique, boulangère

Véronique runs a small country bakery in the west of France with her husband. Her day is complicated by the fact that in thinly populated areas the only way bakers can make a living is to deliver bread to villages and outlying farms. You will see her on a typical day and hear her describing what she does. This will give you a glimpse of the life of French rural areas. The aim of the first *activité* is to give you the opportunity to look closely at the video and listen to the sound-track. You will then concentrate in more detail on what Véronique is saying and pick out some of the key phrases that you will need to learn later on.

Activité 34
20 MINUTES

V I D E O

1   Read the questions below and then watch the video sequence *Véronique, boulangère* (30:33–34:35). You will find most of the answers by looking at the images. Write your answers in French, using complete sentences.

Regardez la vidéo pour trouver les réponses aux questions suivantes.

(a) La camionnette de Véronique est de quelle couleur?

(b) Qu'est-ce qui est écrit au dessus de la porte du dépôt de Brain?

(c) Au dépôt de Brain il y a une étiquette sur le pain. Elle dit de ne pas faire quoi?

(d) La femme qui porte un bébé achète combien de baguettes?

2 Watch the video sequence again and match the following things that Véronique says she does with the time that she does them.

Trouvez les expressions de temps qui correspondent à ce que dit Véronique.

(a) Je me lève

(b) Je pars pour une première livraison

(c) Je reviens ici pour préparer le repas

(d) Nous avons une interruption l'après-midi

(e) Nous rouvrons

(i) à quatre heures.

(ii) de deux heures à quatre heures.

(iii) vers six heures et demie.

(iv) vers onze heures et demie.

(v) vers huit heures et demie.

Saying when something happens: 'vers', 'à', 'de... à...', 'entre... et...'

These words are all used to give information about the timing of events. You heard *vers* and *à* in Book 1 of *Cadences*, where people were talking about what time of year they were going on holiday. They are used in the same way when talking about times of the day.

Vers is used to indicate the approximate time at which something is done. Remember that the 's' at the end of *vers* is not pronounced.

> *Je me lève vers six heures et demie.*
> I get up at about six thirty.

À is used to talk about the exact time at which something is done.

> *Nous rouvrons le magasin à quatre heures.*
> We reopen the shop at four o'clock.

De... à... is used to talk about a period of time during which something takes place. For example, when Véronique was talking about her typical day, she used the following expression:

> *Nous avons une interruption l'après-midi qui est de deux heures à quatre heures.*
> We have a break from two to four.

Notice that *heures* needs to be repeated whenever a time is mentioned, whereas the word 'hours' is often omitted in English. Note, too, that the 's' in *heures* is not pronounced.

Entre... et... is used in a similar way to *de... à...*, but it is used to state the times between which something is done. For example, you could say:

> *Je déjeune entre midi et deux heures.*
> I have lunch between midday and two o'clock.

The following short *activité* will give you practice in using these expressions.

Activité 35

1 0   M I N U T E S

AUDIO 13

1   The first part of this audio extract asks you questions about your daily routine. Answer as indicated, choosing the appropriate expressions. We give you the words and phrases for the various activities below. Go through this exercise a few times until you can do it confidently.

Écoutez l'extrait et répondez de la manière indiquée.

> *Exemple*
> – Quand est-ce que vous travaillez le matin?
> – (From eight until midday.)
> – Je travaille de huit heures à midi.

> ***Pour vous aider***
> *je travaille au bureau*   I work in the office
> *je dîne*   I eat dinner
> *je me lève*   I get up
> *je me couche*   I go to bed
> *je finis mon travail*   I finish work

2   The second part of the extract asks similar questions, but this time there are no suggested answers. Give the answer that applies to you.

Écoutez l'extrait et répondez aux questions. Dites ce qui est vrai pour vous.

Stating purpose: 'pour' + infinitive

Look at the following examples taken from what Véronique said on the video.

> *Je prépare donc le magasin pour ouvrir à huit heures.*

> *Je reviens ici... pour préparer... le repas.*

The preposition *pour*, followed by an infinitive, is used to indicate why something is done. This is an easy expression to use.

Here is another example:

> Je quitte la maison à huit heures pour aller au travail.

You should learn examples of these expressions and perhaps note them in your dossier, making the times and details match your own circumstances.

Colette, éclusière

Colette, the lock-keeper, is employed by her *département* (roughly the equivalent of a county council) to work the lock and generally to help and advise the tourists who pass through. Her day is very different from that of Véronique. From Colette you will learn a number of words and phrases that will improve your ability to talk about your own working day.

Activité 36
20 MINUTES
VIDEO

1 Read the sentences below then watch the video sequence *Colette, éclusière* (34:38–35:53). Tick whether the sentences are true or false. Correct any false ones in French.

Lisez les phrases suivantes puis regardez la vidéo. Cochez vrai ou faux pour chacune et corrigez les phrases fausses en français.

	Vrai	Faux
(a) Colette commence son travail à huit heures.	❑	❑
(b) Elle déjeune entre midi et quatorze heures.	❑	❑
(c) Elle finit sa journée de travail à vingt heures.	❑	❑
(d) Quand Colette n'est pas là les touristes peuvent eux-mêmes actionner l'écluse.	❑	❑

2 Watch the video sequence again if you need to and write down the French for the English phrases listed below.

Trouvez l'équivalent français de chacune des expressions données ci-dessous.

(a) I look after my children.

(b) I start my day at…

(c) I start working again…

(d) I finish it at…

(e) Between midday and two o'clock.

Reflexive verbs

In describing her day Véronique used the reflexive verb *se lever*.

> *Je me lève vers six heures et demie.*
> I get up at about six thirty.

Reflexive verbs are very common in French and we assume you already know how to use them in the present tense. If you are not sure you remember what reflexive verbs are, or their present tense conjugation, look at page 109 in the Grammar Book.

S'occuper de occurs in a wide variety of contexts. The following examples show how it is used and give you some possible English translations.

> *Je m'occupe de mes enfants.*
> I look after my children.

> *Je m'occupe des clients.*
> I deal with the customers.

> *Je m'occupe du magasin.*
> I'm in charge of the shop.

Giving short talks

One thing we ask you to do quite regularly throughout this course is to give a short talk or monologue. You have already done a few. There are certain techniques that you can use to make sure that you gain the maximum benefit from this type of exercise:

1   Make sure you are familiar with the language that leads up to the exercise. You will find it difficult to talk fluently if you are struggling to remember individual words and phrases.

2   Make brief notes so that you have a plan of what you want to say, but don't write down and read out whole sentences as this will make what you say sound artificial and will not give you practice in speaking spontaneously. If you think you need to write down whole phrases, perhaps you should go through the previous *activités* again so that you are more familiar with the language you will be using or spend time memorizing the vocabulary and expressions that you need.

3   Do your talk a number of times. You should find that it gets easier as you go along.

4   When you think you can do it quite freely, record your talk on tape. Listen to yourself and think about the following points:

   •   Is it too fast or too slow? In other words, is it hesitant and jerky, or are you trying to say the things you know well as fast as possible? If you are doing this, the accuracy of your grammar and pronunciation is likely to suffer. Fluency is about talking confidently and in a free-flowing way. It is not about speed, so don't try to talk too fast.

- Do you vary the pitch or is your voice a monotone?

- Can you spot any places where your pronunciation could improve?

The next *activité* gives you the opportunity to put this advice into practice. It should also help you to remember the words and phrases that we have introduced so far in this section.

Activité 37
1 5 MINUTES

Describe a typical day in line with the cues that are given below. The cues are a guide only. Try to include some variety of structures and vocabulary. You should be able to use some of the expressions of time you learned in Book 1 of *Cadences* and earlier in this book (e.g. *d'habitude, des fois, souvent, pendant*). Practise your talk a few times to memorize the phrases and then record yourself.

Racontez en français la journée suivante.

- You get up at about 7.00.

- You look after your children.

- You leave to go to work at 8.30.

- You work from 9.00 to 12.30.

- Between 12.30 and 1.30 you have lunch.

- At 1.30 you start work again.

- You finish your day at 5.30.

In the next *activité* you're going to prepare another short talk about what is a typical day for you, but this time using your own information and describing your own circumstances. You've learned most of the language you need in the previous *activité*, but you may need to use a dictionary to find some extra vocabulary. Once you're happy with what you want to say, record yourself on tape. Then play back your talk and think about the points mentioned in point 4 on the previous page.

Activité 38
1 5 MINUTES

Explain what a typical day's routine is like for you. You could include information about what you do and where you work, and the reasons why you do certain things (use *pour* + infinitive). Record your talk.

Prenez quelques notes puis racontez votre journée habituelle. Donnez une ou deux raisons avec 'pour' et l'infinitif.

La journée d'un pompier

Alain's day is very different from that of Colette or Véronique. As a fire-fighter, he is tied to fairly inflexible as well as extremely busy schedules in the Angers fire station where he works. His description of his typical day will give you practice in listening to a longer recording to pick out specific details.

Activité 39

15 MINUTES

AUDIO 14

2 45

Below are two lists, one of times and another of the various activities that make up the fire-fighter's day. Listen to the audio extract and match the activities with the times at which they occur. Listen to the extract as often as you wish, but you will probably find all the answers after listening two or three times.

Écoutez l'extrait et indiquez l'activité qui correspond à chaque horaire.

1   8–8.30 a.m.   (a) manœuvre
2   9.10–9.30 a.m.   (b) étude du secteur
3   9.30–10 a.m.   (c) pause
4   10–11 a.m.   (d) travaux dans les services
5   11 a.m.–2 p.m.   (e) douche, casse-croûte
6   2–5 p.m.   (f) repos, loisirs et repas
7   5–5.15 p.m.   (g) séance de sport
8   5.15–6 p.m.   (h) repos et loisirs dans la caserne
9   6 p.m.–8 a.m.   (i) vérification du matériel

Pour vous aider

le casse-croûte   the snack (an informal word)

l'étude du secteur   the study of maps of the town (to be able to find places more quickly in an emergency)

la manœuvre   exercises (practice drills, simulated emergencies, etc.)

une séance   a session

dans l'enceinte de   on the premises

la caserne   the fire station (generally this means 'barracks')

Claude, viticulteur

The next video sequence (35:56–38:28) features Claude Papin, a wine grower (*un viticulteur*), talking about his working life. There is no specific learning associated with this sequence, so you can miss it out if you don't have time to study it now. If you do have time, however, you'll find the listening practice useful.

Here is a summary of Claude's year to help you understand what he is saying. You will also find the transcript helpful. Claude's life is dominated not by a daily rhythm but an annual one, that of the seasons. It starts with the grape harvest (*les vendanges*). After that he works in his wine cellar (*la cave*) making the wine (*la vinification*), while other groups of people undertake the tiring job of pruning the vines (*tailler la vigne*). Then comes the business part of his year, his *travail de commerçant*, which is followed by having to deliver (*livrer*) or send off (*expédier*) the wine he has sold. The last tiring job is *l'effeuillage*, which is the thinning out of the new leaves. The final work of ripening the grapes (*la maturité du raisin*) is left to the sunshine.

Durée du travail

So far in this section we've been looking at individual work patterns, but we turn now to the trends in working patterns for French society as a whole. The next *activité* will give you reading and writing practice and help you to extend your vocabulary. You should do the first step of the *activité* before reading the accompanying text.

Activité 40

20 MINUTES

1   Match the words and phrases in the list on the left with the definitions that are given on the right.

Trouvez dans la colonne de droite la définition qui correspond à chaque expression de la colonne de gauche.

(a) évolution sociale   (i)   d'une manière claire

(b) décennie   (ii)   la victoire socialiste aux élections

(c) nettement   (iii) développement de la société

(d) accroissement   (iv)   observer

(e) l'arrivée au pouvoir de   (v)   augmentation
     la gauche
                                        (vi)   période de dix ans
(f) constater

2   *Lisez le texte ci-dessous.*

Durée du travail: toujours moins

La réduction de la durée du travail est l'une des évolutions sociales majeures des dernières décennies. Le temps de travail s'est nettement effacé au profit du temps libre. Mais on a constaté récemment une tendance à l'accroissement du nombre des heures supplémentaires, du fait de l'accroissement de l'activité des entreprises.

Le travail représente 8 années de travail sur 42 années 'éveillées' pour les hommes, 6 années sur 45 pour les femmes.

[...]

... Entre 1969 et 1980, la durée du travail passait de 45,2 heures à 40,8. L'arrivée au pouvoir de la gauche donnait un nouveau coup de pouce: 39 heures en 1982 et la perspective de 35 heures à moyen terme. Un projet d'ailleurs remis en cause depuis.

La réduction constatée est due principalement à la réduction des horaires les plus longs, dans le bâtiment par exemple (où la moyenne atteignait près de 50 heures en 1968) ou dans le secteur agroalimentaire (46 heures en 1968). Dans la pratique, la diminution s'est traduite surtout par un resserrement des journées de travail: les horaires de travail commencent plus tard et finissent plus tôt; l'interruption pour le repas de midi est plus courte.

(Mermet, 1990, pp, 270–2)

Pour vous aider

s'est nettement effacé has clearly diminished

un nouveau coup de pouce a new push in the right direction

à moyen terme in the medium term

un resserrement des journées de travail a shortening of the working day

Durée hebdomadaire moyenne selon la profession (1989, en heures)

	Heures
• Agriculteurs	52,0
• Artisans, commerçants, chefs d'entreprise	51,5
• Professions libérales	45,7
• Employés	36,0
• Ouvriers	38,7

Based on data from INSEE

3   The following sentences summarize parts of the text. Fill in the gaps using the words provided in the box.

Complétez les phrases suivantes avec les mots de l'encadré.

(a) Depuis quelques années, les Français travaillent _____ et se donnent plus de _____ .

(b) Le gouvernement _____ a _____ cette _____ .

(c) À l'avenir, on espère _____ la durée _____ du travail à trente-cinq heures.

> réduire, socialiste, encouragé,
> hebdomadaire, tendance, moins,
> temps libre

4   The table below is designed to encourage you to notice the relationships between words. You are given either a noun or a verb from the text you read in step 2 of this *activité*. Look through the text to find the words needed to complete the table. It is useful to be aware of these relationships (and of course they do not exist only between nouns and verbs, but also between adverbs and adjectives). It's often possible to work out the meaning of a word you meet for the first time because of its relationship to a word you already know.

Trouvez dans le texte les mots qui conviennent pour remplir le tableau.

Nom	*Verbe*
la réduction	réduire
	diminuer
le commencement	
la fin	
la constatation	

3.2 C'est un beau métier?

Our interest shifts now to people's reactions to and feelings about their working lives. We asked various people whether they liked their job: *C'est un beau métier?* Colette and Claude talk about the advantages and disadvantages of their jobs and two employees (*employés*) of Aérospatiale in Nantes explain what constitutes for them *la qualité de la vie au travail.* Jacqueline, the florist, then explains why she is particularly keen on her job. Finally, you will read a text about a rather intriguing source of health problems at work.

As you work through this topic, you will learn how to talk about the advantages and disadvantages of your own situation and some ways of describing the work environment. You will also learn to build sentences with *qui* and *que*.

Avantages et inconvénients

The first audio extract in this topic features Colette and Claude whom we met earlier in this section.

Activité 41

20 MINUTES

AUDIO 15

30 §.

1   Listen to the first part of the audio extract, where Colette lists several advantages to her job. She also mentions one disadvantage (which doesn't seem to concern her too much). In English, give one advantage and one disadvantage of the job according to Colette.

Dans l'Extrait 15, Colette mentionne plusieurs avantages et un inconvénient de son métier. En anglais, citez un des avantages et l'inconvénient.

Pour vous aider

un loyer   a rent

sur mon lieu d'habitation   where I live

la nourrice   the child minder

2   Listen to the second part of the audio extract, then use the words in the box to complete the following statements Claude makes about his job.

Complétez le texte ci-dessous à l'aide des expressions données dans l'encadré.

(a) C'est un métier qui _demande_ beaucoup de passion, beaucoup d'énergie_ .

(b) C'est un _métier_ complet.

(c) C'est _passionat_ , hein le… phénomène de fermentation du vin… un travail de _relation hum_ où on _rencontre_ des tas de _gens_ .

(d) C'est _plaisant_.

(e) On est encore parmi les derniers hommes à vivre _dehors_.

> plaisant, métier, relations humaines, d'énergie,
> passionnant, rencontre, dehors, demande, gens

Talking about advantages and disadvantages

There are a number of useful words and phrases in this short audio extract. For instance, did you notice how to ask about advantages and disadvantages?

> Quels sont les avantages du métier?

> Quels sont les inconvénients du travail?

You can use these expressions to ask about any sort of situation:

> *Quels sont les avantages de la vie à la campagne?*
> What are the advantages of living in the countryside?

> *Quels sont les inconvénients des vacances à l'étranger?*
> What are the disadvantages of holidays abroad?

Colette answered both questions in a similar way:

> Les avantages? C'est que j'ai un logement de fonction.

> Les inconvénients? C'est que je travaille tous les dimanches.

And what are these advantages and disadvantages? Colette has a *logement de fonction*, a house provided by her employer. Another common advantage might be a *voiture de fonction*, a company car (though these are a much less common perk in France than they are in Great Britain). She also has the advantage that she enjoys almost every aspect of her job: *Je n'ai pas vraiment d'inconvénients*.

Here is a list of phrases that you may want to use to describe your own activities:

> *C'est bien payé.*
> It's well paid.

> *C'est passionnant.*
> It's exciting/fascinating.

> *On rencontre beaucoup de gens.*
> You meet lots of people.

> *Il y a toujours trop à faire.*
> There is always too much to do.

> *C'est fatigant.*
> It's tiring.

C'est stressant.
It's stressful.

Je n'ai pas vraiment d'inconvénients.
For me, there aren't any real disadvantages.

In the next *activité* you'll practise talking about advantages and disadvantages.

Listen to the audio extract and answer the questions according to the suggestions given in English. For the last two questions, no answers are suggested. We want you to give your own answers. (If these questions do not apply to your own circumstances, give a short explanation why, just as you would in a real conversation.)

Écoutez l'extrait et répondez aux questions de la manière indiquée. À la fin de l'extrait répondez aux questions sur vos vraies conditions de travail.

— Quels sont les avantages de votre travail?

— (Advantages? You have a company car.)

— Il y a d'autres avantages?

— (You like your job very much.)

— Quels sont les inconvénients de votre travail?

— (Disadvantages? You work every Saturday.)

— Et il y a d'autres inconvénients?

— (You don't really have any bad points.)

— Et vous, personnellement, quels sont les avantages de votre travail?

— Et quels sont les inconvénients?

Le travail, ça me plaît bien

The two people you are now going to hear from work in the hi-tech aviation company Aérospatiale in Nantes, which makes Airbuses. Although they work for a large company, many of the points they make about the *qualité de vie au travail* could apply to many other work situations. From them you will learn some of the words and phrases that can be used to describe a work environment.

The next *activité* gives you practice in summarizing and understanding the main points of a listening passage.

Activité 43

15 MINUTES

AUDIO 17

393

1   Listen to the first interviewee on this audio extract who says that, in addition to having an interesting job, there are two important factors that contribute to the quality of life at work. Write down in English what these two factors are, using some of the examples he gives.

Écoutez le premier employé interviewé. Selon lui, il y a plusieurs facteurs de qualité de la vie dans l'entreprise, par exemple avoir un travail intéressant. Notez en anglais les deux autres facteurs, avec quelques exemples.

2   Listen to the second interviewee. Explain in English whether you think he makes the same points as the previous interviewee.

Écoutez le deuxième employé. Est-ce que cet homme est d'accord avec le premier sur la qualité de la vie au travail?

Pour vous aider

un travail qui vous intéresse   a job that interests you

un atelier   a workshop

bruyant   noisy

un endroit   a place

sale   dirty

le style de direction   the style of management

This audio extract contains the very useful phrase *ça me plaît bien* (I like it a lot). You should recognize this from your work on *Cadences*, Book 1, where you saw the expression *ça m'a beaucoup plu.*

Le métier de fleuriste

Jacqueline, the florist, derives great pleasure from her work. In the next *activité* you will find out why. You will then go on to look in more detail at what she is saying.

Activité 44

15 MINUTES

AUDIO 18

× 60

1   Listen to the audio extract a couple of times to get an overall understanding of what Jacqueline is saying and then list what she sees as the three main requirements of her job.

Écoutez l'extrait plusieurs fois. Selon Jacqueline, il y a trois conditions pour être une bonne fleuriste. Notez-les en anglais.

Pour vous aider

manque de sommeil   lack of sleep

qu'est-ce que je pourrais vous dire?   what could I tell you?

un long apprentissage a long apprenticeship

CAP (le certificat d'aptitude professionnelle) a vocational qualification

des emplois-qualifications periods of work experience (to gain qualified status)

les artisanats small craft industries

2 Listen again to what Jacqueline says and follow it in the transcript below. Fill the gaps with the words provided in the box.

Écoutez de nouveau l'extrait et complétez la transcription suivante avec les mots de l'encadré.

Je suis ____fleuriste____ et je trouve que… enfin, c'est un métier très très très ____passionnant____ . Je suis très amoureuse de mon métier. On a un contact euh… avec la ____nature____ euh… vraiment exceptionnel. C'est un métier très très difficile ____qui____ demande un sens artistique, une bonne santé physique et… , mais, euh, ça compense euh… tous nos problèmes de manque de sommeil et tout ça quand on crée des bouquets. Qu'est-ce que je pourrais vous dire de ce métier? Que ça demande un long ____apprentissage____ , hein, que les employées arrivent en apprentissage et ça dure deux ans pour un CAP. Et après elles ont des emplois-qualifications, ou des stages ____qui____ durent à peu près deux, trois ans. Faut à peu près, pour avoir une bonne ____maîtrise____ de ce métier, entre sept et huit ans comme tous les ____artisanats____ euh, comme ça, de, de fabrication, comme beaucoup, beaucoup de ____métiers____ .

> maîtrise, qui, apprentissage, métiers, fleuriste, passionnant, qui, nature, artisanats

Activité 45
15 MINUTES

1 Look at the sentences below and try to work out why *qui* is used in some places and *que* in others.

Regardez les phrases ci-dessous. Pourquoi utilise-t-on 'qui' dans certaines et 'que' dans d'autres?

(a) Le métier que je fais en ce moment est très intéressant.

(b) C'est un métier très difficile qui demande un sens artistique.

(c) L'apprentissage que j'ai fait pour ce métier a été très long.

(d) Il y a des stages qui durent à peu près deux ans.

2   Now go through the sentences and underline the verb that follows *qui* or *que*. Then underline the subject of those verbs. There is no *corrigé* for this *activité*. The explanation is given below.

Dans chacune des phrases ci-dessus, il y a un verbe après 'qui' et 'que'. Soulignez le verbe et son sujet dans chaque exemple.

Relative pronouns: 'qui', 'que'

Here are the sentences from the previous *activité*. The words you should have underlined are in bold type.

(a) *Le métier que **je fais** en ce moment est très intéressant.*
    The job that I'm doing at the moment is very interesting.

(b) *C'est **un métier** très difficile qui **demande** un sens artistique.*
    It's a difficult job that requires an artistic touch.

(c) *L'apprentissage que **j'ai fait** pour ce métier a été très long.*
    The apprenticeship that I did for this job was very long.

(d) *Il y a **des stages** qui **durent** à peu près deux ans.*
    There are work placements which last about two years.

To know when to use *qui* and when to use *que*, you have to understand the distinction between the subject and the object of a verb. The Study Guide glossary and Section 2 of this book will help you if you need to check.

The verb that follows *que* has a subject with it. In example (a) above, the verb is *fais* and its subject is *je*. On the other hand, in example (b), the verb following *qui* (i.e. *demande*) does not have a subject with it. It is the word *métier* (found before *qui* in the sentence) that is the subject.

Qui replaces the subject of the verb that follows it.

* It is a pronoun which stands for a noun mentioned in the first part of the sentence.

* *Qui* is never shortened.

    C'est une femme qui a beaucoup de responsabilités.

Que replaces the direct object of the verb that follows it.

* It stands for a noun mentioned in the first part of the sentence.

* The verb that follows *que* has a subject with it in that part of the sentence.

* *Que* is shortened to *qu'* when the word that follows begins with a vowel.

    L'apprentissage qu'il fait est difficile.

Both *qui* and *que* can be translated into English by 'who', 'that' or 'which' so, when deciding whether to use *qui* or *que*, it doesn't help to think about what the English equivalent might be. Instead, you need to think about the grammar of the French sentence.

In French *que* is never omitted, but the English equivalents 'that' or 'which' may be left out. For example, take the following sentence:

> Le livre que j'ai acheté hier.

This could be translated as 'the book **that** I bought yesterday' or 'the book I bought yesterday'.

The following *activité* should help you to distinguish between *qui* and *que*.

Activité 46
30 MINUTES

1 Write *qui*, *que* or *qu'* in the following sentences as appropriate. In each case look at the verb following the gap and decide whether it has a subject with it or not.

Complétez les phrases suivantes avec 'qui', 'que' ou 'qu''.

(a) C'est un métier _____ j'aime beaucoup.

(b) C'est un métier _____ a beaucoup d'avantages.

(c) Le pain _____ elle vend est très bon.

(d) Jacqueline est une femme _____ aime beaucoup son travail.

(e) Colette est la femme _____ travaille dans une écluse.

(f) C'est Colette _____ j'ai vue sur la vidéo.

(g) La camionnette _____ elle conduit appartient à l'entreprise.

(h) Claude Papin est un homme _____ fait bien son travail.

(i) C'est quelqu'un _____ travaille beaucoup.

(j) C'est surtout le style de direction _____ je déteste.

2 Translate the following sentences into French, taking care to use *qui* and *que* correctly.

Traduisez les phrases suivantes.

(a) The wine that Claude produced is of very good quality.

(b) I met a man who works in Paris.

(c) It's an excellent wine that I bought in Angers.

(d) The fire-fighter we heard on the cassette is called Alain.

(e) People who like cooking often like reading recipe books.

(f) The *pieds-noirs* are the French people who used to live in Algeria before 1962.

The distinction between *qui* and *que* is an important one: your French will be inaccurate and confusing if you cannot use these words properly. If you are still unsure, read pages 85–6 of the Grammar Book or look back at some of the texts you have read so far and find more examples of the use of *qui* and *que*. Try to decide why *qui* or *que* was used in each case.

La maladie des tours

In considering the advantages and disadvantages of a particular job, people often comment on their work environment. The short text that you're going to read next provides examples of the type of health problem that can arise at work.

Activité 47
15 MINUTES

1 *Lisez le texte 'La maladie des tours'.*

La maladie des tours

Des enquêtes ont montré que les salariés étaient plus souvent absents lorsque leur entreprise emménageait dans des bureaux situés dans un immeuble de grande hauteur. Des troubles fonctionnels respiratoires ou sensoriels, une fatigue plus intense, la somnolence, des difficultés de concentration, des maux de tête, etc., ont été observés, sans qu'on puisse les attribuer avec certitude à une cause objective (en particulier la climatisation). Ces troubles s'estompent dans le temps et sont inexistants chez les jeunes et ceux qui commencent leur carrière dans des bureaux situés dans une tour.

(Mermet, 1990, p. 275)

Pour vous aider

des enquêtes surveys
les salariés the employees
leur entreprise their company
emménageait dans moved into
un immeuble a building
sans qu'on puisse les attribuer without it being possible to ascribe them
s'estompent die down
ceux qui those who

2   *Répondez aux questions suivantes.*

(a) What have the surveys mentioned at the start of the text shown?

(b) Which of the following health problems is mentioned: stomach aches, drowsiness, headaches, nose bleeds?

(c) Are these problems permanent?

(d) What groups are totally unaffected?

3.3 Les femmes et le travail

In France, as in Great Britain, the main burden of child care falls most often on women. This can be especially difficult when a woman works both inside and outside the home. In this topic we look at some of the problems that can arise. You'll learn how to talk about some common household tasks and to say what your rights are.

Liliane, institutrice

Liliane works part time (*à mi-temps*) as a primary school teacher and uses the rest of her time to study at university. As a mother of three children, she knows all about the demands families can make. She does however have help from her husband because he shares the housework (*les travaux du ménage*). Liliane is expecting a fourth child and she knows what benefits (*avantages sociaux*) she has a right to.

Activité 48
30 MINUTES
VIDEO

1   Read the questions below. To answer them, watch the first part of the *Les femmes et le travail* video sequence (38:31–40:00) where Liliane explains her timetable (*emploi du temps*).

Regardez la vidéo pour trouver les réponses aux questions suivantes.

(a) Quand est-ce que Liliane passe ses examens?

(b) Quand est-ce qu'elle va à l'université?

(c) Elle passe combien d'heures par jour à l'université?

(d) Quand est-ce qu'elle va à l'école?

Pour vous aider

je range   I put away

dossiers   files

mon cahier-journal d'institutrice   my teacher's mark and record book

2   In the next part of the sequence (40:01–40:41) Liliane says '*on se partage le travail*' (we share the work, i.e. she and her husband). Liliane gives four examples of the sorts of task that are shared. Look at the list of

possibilities below and guess which four these might be, then watch the video to check whether you are right.

Lisez les tâches ménagères ci-dessous. Liliane mentionne quatre d'entre elles. Devinez lesquelles et regardez la vidéo pour vérifier si vous avez raison.

(a) *faire les courses*   to do the shopping

(b) *faire la vaisselle*   to do the washing up

(c) *préparer les repas*   to do the cooking

(d) *(faire) le ménage*   (to do) the housework

(e) *(faire) la lessive*   (to do) the washing

(f) *s'occuper des enfants*   to look after the children

(g) *passer l'aspirateur*   to do the vacuum-cleaning

3   Liliane then explains why she decided to work part time (*pourquoi je me suis mise à mi-temps*). Read the following possible explanations and then watch the video (40:41–41:20) to decide which one most closely matches what Liliane says.

L'une des phrases suivantes explique correctement pourquoi Liliane s'est mise à travailler à mi-temps. Quelle est cette phrase?

(a) Elle a voulu consacrer plus de temps à ses propres enfants.

(b) Elle a voulu consacrer plus de temps à ses études.

(c) Travailler avec les enfants toute la journée et puis s'occuper d'eux et de la maison le soir, c'est trop fatigant.

(d) Elle n'aime pas tellement son métier, elle s'ennuie au travail.

Pour vous aider

tendu   tense

régler des tas de problèmes   to sort out a host of problems

4   The amount of *congé-maternité* (maternity leave) varies according to how many children you have. Watch the next part of the video sequence (41:21–42:33) and fill in the table below.

Regardez la vidéo et complétez le tableau suivant.

Nombre d'enfants	Durée du congé-maternité

Pour vous aider

enceinte   pregnant

congés-maladie   sick leave

si on n'est pas bien   if you're ill

lorsqu'on   when you

l'accouchement   the birth (confinement)

Passer ses examens

In the commentary on the video you heard that Liliane is taking her exams next week:

> La semaine prochaine, elle passe ses examens.

Passer ses examens means 'to take your exams'. 'To pass an exam' is *réussir à un examen* or *être reçu à un examen*.

Stating your rights: 'avoir droit à'

Look at the following example from the video sequence you have just watched.

> **On a droit à** *six mois... de congé-maternité.*
> We're entitled to six months... of maternity leave.

You have heard the expression *avoir droit à* several times. It means 'to have a right to' or 'to be entitled to'. The verb *avoir* changes to agree with its subject.

> **J'ai droit à** *six semaines de congés payés.*
> I'm entitled to six weeks' paid holiday.

Maternity leave and paid holidays are not, of course, the only things that people have a right to at work.

> *J'ai droit à vingt minutes de pause-café le matin.*
> I'm entitled to a twenty-minute coffee break in the morning.

> *À midi, on a droit à une heure pour déjeuner.*
> At midday, we're entitled to an hour for lunch.

The following *activité* will give you some practice at stating what you are entitled to, using *avoir droit à*.

Activité 49
10 MINUTES
AUDIO 19
4 88.

In this audio extract you are asked a number of questions. Answer in the way that is indicated. The last two questions are open-ended and give you chance to talk about your own conditions at work. If these questions do not fit your circumstances, say why.

Écoutez l'extrait et répondez aux questions de la manière indiquée. À la fin de l'extrait, répondez aux questions sur vos vraies conditions de travail.

en passant » » » »

Liliane uses the phrase *Vive le progrès social!* to express her satisfaction with the fact that she's going to benefit from six months' maternity leave. This phrase doesn't translate very easily into English. Strictly speaking, it means

'Long live social progress', but it's difficult to imagine an English speaker actually saying that. In France *Vive le roi* was the equivalent of 'Long live the king' in English. It is quite common in French to use *vive* or *vivent* to express your enthusiasm or support for something. For example, you could say *Vivent les vacances*. In broad terms, *le progrès social* refers to the gradual improvements in the welfare state and the protection it gives to its citizens in terms of benefits and so on.

Over the last 200 years the French population has declined relative to that of other European countries. In 1800 the French population was roughly equivalent to that of Russia, the largest country in Europe. This relative decline caused great political concern during the nineteenth and early twentieth centuries, mainly because a nation's military power was closely related to the size of its population. Measures were taken, therefore, to promote population growth, with the result that the French state is relatively generous in terms of child benefits, maternity provision and so on.

La course contre la montre

You are going to read a letter to a friend from a woman whose husband is not a *nouveau père* (new man) like Liliane's partner and does very little to help. As a consequence, she has to do housework at home in the evening after being at work all day (*faire la double journée*). Racing against the clock (*la course contre la montre*) dominates her life.

'You should try to find a moment to relax ...'

1   *Lisez la lettre puis répondez en français aux questions qui suivent.*

Chère Solange,

Merci de ton petit mot. Je t'ai promis des nouvelles et je cherche depuis trois mois l'occasion de prendre mon stylo pour t'en donner. Enfin, ce soir (minuit moins le quart !), je peux tenir ma promesse ...

Ma vie est une perpétuelle course contre la montre. Je rentre le soir après une longue journée de travail, et je fais la double journée, alors que Yannick, lui, se met dans son fauteuil pour regarder la télé. Il est vrai qu'il va chercher les enfants chez la nourrice au sortir de son bureau, et qu'il les ramène à la maison. Mais c'est à peu près tout !

Après, à moi d'explorer le contenu du frigo pour inventer un menu, et de préparer le dîner. Pendant que les spaghetti cuisent, il faut mettre les deux bambins au lit. Heureusement que la nounou les a déjà nourris, baignés et mis en pyjama. Ensuite, on mange et puis il faut faire la vaisselle, ranger la cuisine et vérifier les affaires de tout le monde pour le lendemain. Tout ça, devine qui le fait pendant que Yannick regarde tranquillement la fin des infos ?

Au début de notre mariage, je croyais pouvoir partager les tâches ménagères avec Yannick. Quelle désillusion ! Les nouveaux maris ? Les nouveaux pères ? Je ne connaît pas ! Enfin, je ne veux pas t'ennuyer plus longtemps avec mes histoires. Et toi, comment vas-tu ? Écris ou téléphone, ça me fera plaisir d'avoir de tes nouvelles.

A très bientôt j'espère, grosses bises,

Marion

Pour vous aider

ton petit mot   your note (short letter)

des nouvelles   news (when talking about a news programme, *les infos* is more common)

la nourrice   the child minder (can also mean nanny)

du frigo   of the fridge (a relaxed way of saying this)

les deux bambins   the two kids

la nounou   the child minder (baby word)

les a déjà nourris   has already fed them

devine   guess

des infos   the news (TV or radio programme)

ça me fera plaisir d'avoir de tes nouvelles   I look forward to hearing all your news

(a) Pour Yannick, s'occuper des enfants se limite à quoi?

(b) Que fait la nourrice pour aider Marion?

(c) Que fait Yannick pendant que Marion s'occupe des enfants?

2   *Cherchez dans le texte l'équivalent français des mots et expressions qui suivent:*

(a) share the housework

(b) make the dinner

(c) I come home

(d) tidy the kitchen

(e) pick up the children

(f) the child minder has already fed and bathed them

(g) he brings them home

(h) the spaghetti is cooking

3   Not all men are as unhelpful as Yannick. Rewrite the second and third paragraphs as if the letter were from a woman whose husband is a *nouveau mari* and does his fair share of the work. Make as many changes as you wish. Some will be quite simple, such as making some of the statements negative instead of positive (e.g. *il ne regarde pas la télé*), or vice versa. Say what things he does and what things they share.

Changez le deuxième et le troisième paragraphe de la lettre pour rendre l'attitude du mari plus positive.

The next *activité* gives you practice at listening to and reproducing the sound [j], which is pronounced like the 'y' of 'yes'. It is a common sound in French and you have already met it many times on the Activities Cassette associated with this book.

Activité 51

5 MINUTES

AUDIO 20/21

1   Listen to the three sentences on Audio Extract 20 and underline the vowels corresponding to each [j] sound.

Écoutez les trois phrases de l'Extrait 20 et soulignez la voyelle qui correspond au son [j] à chaque fois que vous l'entendez.

(a) Le mariage de Liliane a eu lieu hier.

(b) C'est bien fatigant, de cueillir des raisins au soleil.

(c) Yannick bâille, il manque de sommeil.

2   Now play Audio Extract 21, repeating each sentence in the gap that has been left.

Écoutez l'Extrait 21 et répétez les phrases pendant les pauses.

Checking your own written work

One skill we want you to develop as you work through these materials is the ability to check your own written work. Whenever you have done a piece of written work, read it several times, each time concentrating on one aspect only: for instance, gender, singular and plural agreement, verb endings, spelling. Then read it again with a specific question in mind, for example:

- Have I used imperfect tenses appropriately?

- Have I phrased questions accurately?

- Did I think of using a direct object pronoun whenever possible?

- Did I remember to shorten *le* and *la* to *l'* or *de* to *d'* before a noun beginning with a vowel?

- Did I distinguish correctly between *qui* and *que*?

Any one of the points of grammar mentioned in the book can become a focus for re-reading. This way you can evaluate your acquisition of one language point at a time and you are less likely to let errors slip through.

Activité 52

25 MINUTES

We want you to imagine that you have received a letter from a French friend asking you about your life and especially your working life. Write a letter of about 150 words incorporating as much as possible of the language you have learned in this section. In particular, say what your daily routine is, whether you enjoy what you do and what the advantages and disadvantages of your situation are. Add some reasons why you do certain things (*pour* + infinitive). Mention any family responsibilities you have and say what housework you do and when you do it. Make sure you use *qui* and *que* a few times.

Obviously, we cannot give you a *corrigé* for this *activité*, so it will be up to you to check your work for errors. Go through it several times, each time looking for a different type of mistake. For instance, if you find that one of your common mistakes is to forget to make adjectives agree, go through what you have written, concentrating solely on the adjectives. Then, check the verbs: are they in the correct tense, is that tense formed correctly, and do the verbs agree with their subject? You could also refer to Section 1 of this book and to Section 1 of *Cadences*, Book 1, to check on specific features of letter writing.

Écrivez à un ami une lettre de 150 mots qui explique votre routine quotidienne.

Faites le bilan

When you have finished this section of the book, you should be able to:

* State the times at which something happens, both exactly and approximately (*Activités 35* and *37*).

* Use *pour* + infinitive to indicate the reason why something is done (*Activité 38*).

* Give a short talk describing a typical working day (*Activités 37* and *38*).

* Discuss the advantages and disadvantages of a job (*Activité 42*).

* Use *qui* and *que* to construct sentences (*Activité 46*).

* Say what your rights are using *avoir droit à* (*Activité 49*).

* Recognize and pronounce the sound [j] (*Activité 51*).

Vocabulaire à retenir

3.1 Les horaires

un horaire

un viticulteur, une viticultrice

une camionnette

une étiquette

une livraison

au bureau

commencer sa journée à 8/10 heures

reprendre son service

finir sa journée à 17/19 heures

une pause

une séance

le repos

l'étude

un casse-croûte

les vendanges

une cave

livrer

nettement

le pouvoir

une augmentation

la durée hebdomadaire du travail

une réduction

une diminution

un agriculteur, une agricultrice

un chef d'entreprise, une femme chef d'entreprise

un ouvrier, une ouvrière

3.2 C'est un beau métier?

un loyer

une nourrice

un métier

passionnant, e

travailler/jouer dehors

ça me plaît bien

j'ai un travail qui m'intéresse

un atelier

bruyant, e

un endroit

une maison/un métier sale

le manque de sommeil

un apprentissage

l'artisanat

la maîtrise

une enquête

un salarié, une salariée

une entreprise

3.3 Les femmes et le travail

les travaux du ménage

un avantage social, des avantages sociaux

un emploi du temps

ranger

un dossier

consacrer du temps à quelqu'un

tendu, e

régler

être enceinte

un congé de maternité, un congé-maternité

un congé de maladie, un congé-maladie

on n'est/je ne suis pas bien

lorsque

un accouchement

faire la double journée

partager les tâches ménagères

ramener quelqu'un à la maison

nourrir un enfant

Corrigés

Section 1

Activité 1

1 (a) To sail or to go sailing (*une voile* is a sail).

(b) To swim or to go swimming.

(c) To jog or to go jogging. *Footing* is a word used mainly by the younger generation. Other people say *faire de la course*.

(d) To ride or to go horse-riding.

(e) To do body-building or weight-training.

(f) To windsurf or to go windsurfing.

(g) To run (*courir* is to run, e.g. after a bus; *faire de la course* is to run for fitness or in a competition).

(h) To read comic books or comic strips. *Une bande* is a strip; *dessiner* is to draw.

(i) To fish or to go fishing (or angling).

Activité 2

2 The pattern of ticks is as follows:

(a) ✔✔ Marie-Noëlle says *un peu de footing* and Éric says *du footing*. This illustrates the rule on page 219 in your Grammar Book about *du, de la, des* with expressions of quantity.

(b) ✔✔✔

(c) ✔✔ Éric and Stéphane say *beaucoup de sport* and *un peu de sport* respectively. Here again, as you saw at the beginning of Book 1 of *Cadences*, *de* is widely used with expressions of quantity.

Hobbies (d) to (i) are mentioned once each.

3 (a) Stéphane is less sporty. His activities are more varied than Éric's.

(b) It helps him take his mind off his work.

4 (a) Éric;

(b) Stéphane;

(c) Brother Marc;

(d) Éric;

Marie-Noëlle n'a pas donné de précisions.

Activité 4

2 Une fois par semaine; tous les vendredis soirs; de temps en temps.

3 Mais; par exemple; et puis.

4   Here is one possible answer:

> Cher Benoît,
>
> Un petit bonjour de [wherever you live].
>
> Depuis que je suis rentré, je suis très pris par mes enfants. Mais j'ai quand même décidé de m'occuper de moi! Par exemple, je vais au cinéma une fois par mois et je fais de la natation tous les jeudis matins. Et puis de temps en temps, je vais à la mer avec la voiture* pour découvrir la côte.
>
> Tout ça fait énormément d'activités, parfois un peu trop! Mais autrement, tout va bien, le moral est bon. J'espère qu'il en va de même pour toi!
>
> Je t'embrasse,**
>
> Arthur
>
> * Notice that French uses *avec la voiture* (or *en voiture*), whereas in English you would say 'in the car'.
>
> **As you can see, kissing (on paper and in reality) is acceptable between men friends.

In reading through your work, check the following points:

- Did you remember to write *cher* for a man, *chère* for a woman?
- If you're a man, did you also remember to use masculine forms when writing about yourself?

Activité 5

2   (a) It is the best way of rediscovering nature, experiencing a different pace of life and rediscovering the true taste of things.

(b) It was an inexpensive pastime when he was a student without much money; it helped him unwind after his exams.

3   (a) Alors qu'il était étudiant.

(b) Il n'avait pas de gros moyens financiers.

(c) C'est une façon idéale de décompresser.

(d) Depuis une trentaine d'années.

Activité 6

This is how Maurice would probably have answered:

1   Pédestre.

2   Plus de 50 fois.

3   Quelques heures.

4   Seul.

5   If he ticked anything at all here, it would be *jumelles* (with which to contemplate nature).

6   He probably ticked *oui* for the first two.

Activité 7

2 (a) C'est une façon idéale de rester en forme.

(b) C'est trop compétitif pour moi.

(c) C'est le meilleur moyen de se détendre.

(d) C'est juste pour s'amuser.

3 Here are two possible answers. The first one assumes that you are a woman, and the second one a man.

Moi, quand je suis fatiguée, j'aime m'occuper de moi et écouter des cassettes de musique classique. À mon avis, c'est la meilleure façon de se détendre et de découvrir de nouveaux horizons.

Le sport ne me dit rien. Ce n'est pas une chose qui me passionne parce que, d'après moi, c'est trop compétitif. Quand je rentre le soir, je préfère lire. Cela suffit à mon bonheur, parce que je me retrouve tout seul avec mes pensées.

Activité 8

2 Marie-Thérèse likes riding a bicycle (*je fais du vélo*), jogging (*je fais de la course*), doing gymnastics (*je fais de la gymnastique*), body-building (*de la musculation*) and reading (*je lis*). Therefore her obvious choices will be (b), (e) and (f). Note also her use of *du, de la* and *des*. As well as the above, she says '*j'aime… faire **du** sport*', '*je fais… un genre **d**'aérobic*' and '*je fais **de la** course*'.

3 The clue in the language is that they say *tu* to each other. The other clue is logical: if they knew each other well, Marie-Lise would know which hobbies Marie-Thérèse has!

Activité 9

2 Your ride takes you from Les Sièges to Citry (the name which Marie-Lise couldn't remember), then right on to the D117, then right again on to the D310.

Activité 11

1 alors ✔✔✔✔; bien sûr ✔✔✔; eh bien (*or* bien *or* ben) ✔✔.

Activité 13

You should have ticked phrases (c) and (d), and (g) and (h).

Activité 14

You should have ticked *prom'nons-nous, il nous mangerait* and *il nous mang'ra pas*.

Activité 15

1 Jouarre, c'est joli, mais malheureusement la voiture est **indispensable**. C'est un peu moins **cher** qu'à Vincelles, mais il n'y a pas grand-chose à faire. L'avantage, quand même, c'est que le coin est très **calme**. Et puis la maison est **indépendante**, donc il n'y a pas de propriétaire sur place. Il habite à douze kilomètres du gîte.

2   You should have ticked as follows, for these reasons:

   (a) Jouarre (because it has a private bathroom: *une salle de bains particulière*).

   (b) Vincelles (because it has central heating: *le chauffage central*).

   (c) Jouarre (because you will not have to pay for a separate room for your child, but you can have a cot set up in the double bedroom for an extra 45 F).

Activité 16   The conversation should have gone like this:

–   Vous êtes où, là?

–   (At Saint-Potan, it's a farmhouse near Matignon.)

–   À Saint-Potan, c'est une ferme près de Matignon.

–   C'est bien comme gîte?

–   (It's not bad. Very quiet.)

–   C'est pas mal. Très calme.

–   Et qu'est-ce qu'il y a comme possibilités de loisirs dans la région?

–   (Not very much. One can go fishing and go to the swimming pool, and that's all.)

–   Pas grand-chose. On peut pêcher et aller à la piscine et c'est tout.

–   La piscine? Ça vous permet d'occuper les enfants, en tout cas!

–   (No, unfortunately it's 12 kms from here.)

–   Non, malheureusement elle est à douze kilomètres d'ici.

–   Alors vous n'y allez pas?

–   (Yes, from time to time, but in the car.)

–   Si, de temps en temps, mais avec la voiture.

–   C'est pas vraiment idéal, si je comprends bien?

–   (Yes, there are nice walks to be had all the same.)

–   Si, quand même, il y a de belles balades à faire.*

–   Eh bien, alors, bonne fin de séjour!

* You could also have put *quand même* between *il y a* and *de*.

Activité 17   1   (a) Saint-Savinien offers a swimming club for babies and swimming tuition for children, as well as a 10% discount on water-skiing for teenagers and on family fishing permits.

   (b) In Parrigny people who are not so young can do a gentle walk for about an hour at La Hariette.

   (c) Parrigny would suit a single person because its tennis club is organized to find playing partners for those who come on their own. Also, the riding school at Cloiry offers accommodation for single people and individual tuition.

2 Personnellement, je préfère aller dans la région de Parrigny parce que c'est un joli coin avec une forêt et que j'aime retrouver la nature quand je peux m'échapper. Saint-Savinien, ça ne me dit rien parce qu'il y a trop d'eau. C'est sans doute très bien pour les enfants, mais moi, je ne sais pas nager!

Activité 18   1 grave; 2 le travail; 3 une famille; 4 les vacances.

Activité 19   The first possible answer is:

Autrefois, la pêche était un passe-temps réservé aux hommes, et la majorité d'entre eux avait plus de trente ans. Ils se retrouvaient au bord de l'eau, soit à l'aube avant le travail, soit les soirs d'été. En effet, il ne faut pas oublier que 'le week-end' n'existait pas à cette époque. C'étaient des pêcheurs sérieux, qui partageaient silencieusement la même passion. Aujourd'hui, on va à la pêche en famille, avec femme et enfants, surtout pour profiter d'un après-midi au soleil.

The second possibility is: 1, 8, 5, 6, 2, 3, 4, 7, 9.

Activité 20   Autrefois, je sortais beaucoup; j'allais au cinéma toutes les semaines, soit le soir, soit l'après-midi, avec une copine. Au contraire, aujourd'hui je regarde la télévision avec les enfants, surtout pour profiter d'une soirée en famille. En effet, je travaille beaucoup et je ne peux pas être souvent avec eux.

Activité 21   1   –   Il y a la possibilité de pratiquer des activités physiques par ici?
–   (Yes, there is a gym not far from the town.)
–   Oui, il y a une salle de sport* pas loin de la ville.
–   Et qu'est-ce qu'ils proposent comme sports?
–   (All sorts of interesting things.)
–   Plein de choses intéressantes.
–   On peut faire quoi, par exemple?
–   (Well, gymnastics, weight-training, badminton.)
–   Eh bien, de la gymnastique, de la musculation, du badminton.
–   Tiens du badminton, c'est pas mal. On prend une inscription ensemble?
–   (No, it doesn't appeal to you.)
–   Non, ça ne me dit rien.
–   Ah bon, pourquoi?
–   (Because it's indoors. You'd rather be outside and go fishing.)
–   Parce que c'est en salle. J'aime mieux être dehors et aller à la pêche.
–   La pêche? Mais c'est plutôt réservé aux hommes, ça?

* You could also have said *il y a un gymnase pas loin de la ville*.

- (Not at all! It's the ideal way to spend a week-end with a friend!)
- Pas du tout! C'est la façon idéale de partager un week-end avec une copine.
- Mais il faut se lever à l'aube, c'est un peu fatigant, non?
- (Of course, but it's worth it!)
- Bien sûr! Mais ça en vaut la peine!

2   Here are some possible translations:

(a) The advantage of going to Saint-Savinien is that you can enrol for one-to-one tennis lessons.

(b) When I choose a place to rent for the holidays, I prefer a cottage standing on its own.

(c) I started sailing when I was very well off and I carry on because I find it very exciting.

(d) There are some beautiful cycle rides to be had in the area around the gîte.

(e) In the past, fishing was something men did together, mainly on Sundays at dawn. Nowadays, entire families can enjoy a different pace of life by the side of the river.

3   (a) Gilbert faisait beaucoup de footing avant l'accident.

(b) Tous les soirs, on faisait de la musculation au gymnase.
or
Tous les soirs, nous faisions de la musculation au gymnase.

(c) Quand tu partais en vacances, est-ce que tu emportais beaucoup de livres?
or
Quand tu partais en vacances, emportais-tu beaucoup de livres? (A more formal way of asking.)
or
Quand tu partais en vacances, tu emportais beaucoup de livres? (More suitable for asking the question orally, with a rising intonation at the end.)

Section 2

| Activité 22 | |

1   Philippe talks about his special car, his model car collection and his father's collection of comic books.

2   When I got my car it completely changed my life, it gave me a lot of freedom. I got my car three years ago. It has been specially adapted for me.

3   J'ai eu (infinitive *avoir*); elle a été (infinitive *être*).

Activité 23

2 (a) **Livres** et vieux **documents** (masculine plural).

(b) **Appareils-photos** (masculine plural).

(c) **Collection** de modèles réduits (feminine singular).

3 (a) Le volume 1 de la série *Monseigneur le Vin*.

(b) La bibliothèque.

(c) La cheminée marbre style Louis XV.

(d) Les cartes postales.

Activité 24

1 (a) feminine singular; (b) masculine singular; (c) masculine plural; (d) feminine plural; (e) masculine singular.

2 (a) La bibliothèque, vous la vendez combien?

(b) L'album, vous le vendez combien?

(c) Les lits, vous les vendez combien?

(d) Les machines à coudre, vous les vendez combien?

(e) Le magazine, vous le vendez combien?

3 (a) D'accord, la bibliothèque, je l'achète.

(b) Dans ce cas, l'album de photos, je l'achète.

(c) Eh bien oui, les lits jumeaux, je les achète.

(d) Elles sont bon marché, les machines à coudre: je les achète.

Activité 25

1 (b) les; (c) les; (d) la.

2 – Tu as un nombre phénoménal de bandes dessinées!

– (Yes, you bought them cheap.)

– Oui, je les ai achetées bon marché.

– Et les cartes postales, tu les as eues comment?

– (Well, you found them in an antique shop.)

– Eh bien, je les ai trouvées chez un antiquaire.

– Il paraît que tu as aussi une magnifique collection de modèles réduits?

– (Yes, but unfortunately you're selling them.)

– Oui, mais malheureusement, je les vends.

– Tu les vends combien?

– (It depends. When they're in good condition, they're worth a lot.)

– Ça dépend. Quand ils sont en bon état, ils valent très cher.

– Et celle-ci, la Citroën miniature, tu la vends aussi?

– (No never! It is of great sentimental value to you.)

– Non, jamais! Elle a une grande valeur sentimentale pour moi!

If you had a problem with *je l'ai acheté/je l'ai trouvé*, this might be a good point to revise the formation of the perfect tense (see Book 1 of *Cadences*).

3 Here are two possible answers: the first contains a masculine noun in the first sentence; the second a feminine noun.

(a) J'ai **un** bijou qui a une grande valeur sentimentale pour moi.

(b) Je l'ai **trouvé** chez un antiquaire.

(c) Je l'ai **acheté** cher.

(d) J'ai quand même l'intention de **le** vendre un jour si j'ai besoin d'argent.

or

(a) J'ai **une** paire de chaussures de marche qui a une grande valeur sentimentale pour moi.

(b) Je l'ai **trouvée** dans un magasin de sport.

(c) Je l'ai **achetée** bon marché.

(d) J'ai l'intention de **la** garder toujours.

Activité 26

2 pendant ce temps, puis, ensuite, quand, d'abord, une fois qu'.

3 Picture 1, caption (e); picture 2, caption (c); picture 3, caption (a); picture 4, caption (b); picture 5, caption (d). Here is the complete recipe in the correct order:

Veau jardinière

Ingrédients pour six personnes

1,5 kg de veau
2 kg de petits pois frais
500 g d'oignons blancs
500 g de carottes
4 petits navets
du persil
du beurre
du sel
du poivre
une feuille de laurier
2 morceaux de sucre
de l'huile
2 litres d'eau pour le bouillon
un grand récipient

Choisissez du veau de seconde qualité. Il est beaucoup moins cher que l'escalope, mais pour faire à la jardinière, il est tout aussi délicieux.

D'abord, coupez la viande en morceaux. Faites-la revenir dans un peu d'huile. Une fois qu'elle est dorée, mettez-la dans un grand récipient avec un peu de sel, de poivre, une feuille de laurier et un bouquet de persil.

Ensuite, couvrez avec de l'eau bouillante. Mettez sur feu doux. Laissez cuire, avec un couvercle, environ une heure et demie.

Pendant ce temps, épluchez les carottes et les navets. Écossez les petits pois frais. Coupez tous les légumes en petits morceaux, mais laissez les oignons entiers.

Puis mélangez les légumes et ajoutez-les au bouillon, avec deux morceaux de sucre. Remettez le couvercle. Finissez la cuisson à feu très doux.

Quand le veau est presque prêt, enlevez le persil et rajoutez un petit peu de beurre.

Servez bien chaud.

Si vous souhaitez adopter une variante rapide, faites cuire 15 minutes dans l'autocuiseur. Ce plat est exquis à la saison des petits pois frais, et on l'apprécie également réchauffé. Accompagnez-le d'une salade de cœurs de laitue.

Activité 27

Question	Bon, j'ai la viande, je commence par faire quoi?
Réponse	D'abord, **coupe-la** en morceaux.
Question	Et après?
Réponse	**Fais-la revenir** dans un peu d'huile.
Question	Et quand elle est revenue?
Réponse	Une fois qu'elle est dorée, **mets-la** dans un grand récipient.
Question	Combien de temps je la laisse cuire?
Réponse	**Laisse-la cuire**, avec un couvercle, environ une heure et demie.
Question	Et qu'est-ce que je fais pendant qu'elle cuit?
Réponse	Pendant ce temps, **épluche** les carottes et les navets. **Écosse** les petits pois frais.
Question	Qu'est-ce que je fais de tous ces légumes?
Réponse	**Coupe-les** en petits morceaux, mais **laisse** les oignons entiers.
Question	Et puis?
Réponse	Puis **mélange** les légumes et **ajoute-les** au bouillon, avec deux morceaux de sucre. **Remets** le couvercle. **Finis** la cuisson à feu très doux.

Activité 28

2 The *pieds-noirs* are French people who settled in Algeria when it was being colonised in the nineteenth century and left for France at the time of the colony's independence.

3 *Un surnom* is a nickname, while a surname is *un nom de famille*.

4 Yes, with the spread of Asian cooking from 1950 onwards.

5   You should have underlined the following past participles (we show them here followed by the infinitive of the verb to which they relate):

> arrivées (arriver); rapatriées (rapatrier); établis (établir); proposé (proposer); dû (devoir); nés (naître); resté (rester); utilisé (utiliser); influencées (influencer); épicées (épicer); appelées (appeler); spécialisés (spécialiser); ouvert (ouvrir); connu (connaître); devenu (devenir).

Activité 29

2   (a) When there is a party, special occasion or festival.

(b) With the traditional method you start the night before by marinating the meat.

3   The direct object pronouns Henri used are in bold type:

> ... Alors, il y a de l'agneau et du poulet que l'on débite en morceaux pour **les** faire revenir avec de l'oignon... Et une fois que les viandes sont revenues, on **les** met... on **les** allonge dans un bouillon dans lequel on rajoute les légumes qui sont ici... Eh bien, maintenant, je vais préparer donc les légumes. Alors, je vais éplucher les carottes, les navets, les courgettes, je vais écosser les fèves et ensuite, **les** couper en morceaux pour **les** rajouter au bouillon.

If you are still not sure why the *les* in bold type are direct object pronouns while the other *les* are articles, check carefully which *les* are followed by a noun and which are not. Remember, a pronoun stands for a preceding noun, so it will not be followed by a noun.

Activité 30

1   (a) Pendant l'année 1988 75% des Français ont écouté la radio tous les jours ou presque.

(b) Pendant l'année 1988 7% des Français ont joué de la musique régulièrement ou parfois.

(c) Pendant l'année 1988 31% des Français ont lu au moins un livre par mois.

(d) Pendant l'année 1988 64% des Français ont reçu des parents ou des amis pour un repas au moins une fois par mois.

2   (a) Le nombre de gens qui reçoivent des parents ou des amis pour un repas au moins une fois par mois a augmenté.

(b) La proportion des lecteurs de quotidiens a diminué.

(c) Le nombre des téléspectateurs a augmenté.

(d) Le pourcentage de gens qui pratiquent le jardinage a diminué.

Activité 31

1   Au cours de l'année 1988, on constate que 82% des Français **ont regardé** la télévision tous les jours ou presque, contre 42% qui **ont lu** un quotidien et 75% qui **ont écouté** la radio. De plus, 64 % **ont reçu** des parents ou des amis pour un repas au moins une fois par mois. 79% **ont lu** une revue ou un magazine régulièrement et 31% un livre au moins une

fois par mois. Enfin, 12% **ont réparé** une voiture avec plaisir. Pour l'année 1988, on n'a pas de statistiques sur la proportion de gens qui regardent régulièrement des vidéos au magnétoscope. D'une manière générale, on peut dire que les Français pratiquent beaucoup de loisirs à domicile, et notamment des loisirs culturels.

2   For the year 1988, we do not have any figures showing how many people regularly watch videos on a video recorder. In general it can be said that the French are keen on leisure pursuits based in the home, and cultural pursuits in particular.

Activité 32   You could have said something like this:

Au cours de l'année dernière, j'ai reçu des parents ou des amis pour un repas de temps en temps. J'ai lu au moins un livre par semaine et j'ai regardé la télévision régulièrement. Enfin, j'ai écouté la radio tous les jours.

Activité 33   1   This is how your dialogue should have gone.

– Et pour bien connaître les environs?

– (Do some walking!)

– Faites de la randonnée!

– Pour regarder vos films préférés quand vous voulez?

– (Buy a video recorder!)

– Achetez un magnétoscope!

– Pour passer quelques jours dans un endroit calme?

– (Rent a gîte!)

– Louez un gîte!

– Pour passer une bonne soirée au coin du feu?

– (Invite some friends and make a fondue!)

– Invitez des copains* et faites une fondue!

– Et pour se détendre après le travail?

– (Read a cartoon book!)

– Lisez une bande dessinée!

* You could have said *copines*, if you were thinking of an all-female group of friends.

2   (a) 42% des Français lisent un quotidien tous les jours.

(b) Je cuisine pour le plaisir. J'aime recevoir des parents ou des amis pour un repas.

(c) Les Français d'Algérie ont reçu le surnom de 'pieds-noirs'.

(d) Faites attention, une chaise ancienne comme ça, ça vaut très cher!

(e) On a reçu des amis le mois dernier.

(f) Achète les livres, ils les vendent bon marché.

(g) Ça a complètement changé ma vie, il faut le dire!

Section 3

Activité 34

1 (a) Elle est blanche.

(b) Il y a un panneau qui porte le mot 'alimentation'.

(c) Elle dit de ne pas toucher au pain.

(d) Elle achète une baguette.

2 (a) Je me lève vers six heures et demie.

(b) Je pars pour une première livraison vers huit heures et demie.

(c) Je reviens ici pour préparer le repas vers onze heures et demie.

(d) Nous avons une interruption l'après-midi de deux heures à quatre heures.

(e) Nous rouvrons à quatre heures.

Activité 35

– Quand est-ce que vous travaillez le matin?

– (From eight until midday.)

– Je travaille de huit heures à midi.

– À quelle heure est-ce que vous vous couchez?

– (Around eleven thirty.)

– Je me couche vers onze heures et demie.

– Quand est-ce que vous finissez votre travail?

– (Between five and six.)

– Je finis mon travail entre cinq heures et six heures.

– À quelle heure est-ce que vous mangez le soir?

– (Between seven and seven thirty.)

– Je mange entre sept heures et sept heures et demie.

– Quand est-ce que vous vous levez le matin?

– (About seven o'clock.)

– Je me lève vers sept heures.

– Quand est-ce que vous travaillez l'après-midi?

– (From two until five.)

– Je travaille de deux heures à cinq heures.

Activité 36

1 (a) Faux: elle commence son travail à neuf heures.

(b) Vrai.

(c) Vrai.

(d) Faux: les touristes ne peuvent pas actionner eux-mêmes l'écluse.

2 (a) Je m'occupe de mes enfants.

(b) Je commence ma journée à…

(c) Je reprends mon service…

(d) Je la finis à… (notice that 'it' is translated by *la* here because Colette is talking about her day – *ma journée* – which is feminine).

(e) Entre midi et deux heures.

Activité 37

Je me lève vers sept heures. Je m'occupe de mes enfants. Après, je quitte la maison à huit heures et demie pour aller au travail. Je travaille à partir de neuf heures et je continue jusqu'à midi et demie. Pendant la matinée, je m'occupe du magasin. Entre midi et demie et une heure et demie, je déjeune. À une heure et demie, je reprends mon service. Vers le milieu de l'après-midi, je prends un café. D'habitude, je finis ma journée à cinq heures et demie.

Activité 39

1(i), 2(e), 3(b), 4(a), 5(f), 6(d), 7(c), 8(g), 9(h).

Activité 40

1   (a)(iii), (b)(vi), (c)(i), (d)(v), (e)(ii), (f)(iv).

3   (a) Depuis quelques années, les Français travaillent **moins** et se donnent plus de **temps libre**.

(b) Le gouvernement **socialiste** a **encouragé** cette **tendance**.

(c) À l'avenir, on espère **réduire** la durée **hebdomadaire** du travail à trente-cinq heures.

4

Nom	*Verbe*
la réduction	réduire
la diminution	diminuer
le commencement	commencer
la fin	finir
la constatation	constater

Activité 41

1   You could have selected one of these advantages: she works in her own home; she doesn't pay rent because her house comes with the job; she can look after her children while she's working so they don't have to be minded by someone else. The disadvantage is that she works on Sundays.

2   (a) C'est un métier qui **demande** beaucoup de passion, beaucoup **d'énergie**.

(b) C'est un **métier** complet.

(c) C'est **passionnant**, hein le… phénomène de fermentation du vin… un travail de **relations humaines** où on **rencontre** des tas de gens.

(d) C'est **plaisant**.

(e) On est encore parmi les derniers hommes à vivre **dehors**.

Activité 42
- – Quels sont les avantages de votre travail?
- – (Advantages? You have a company car.)
- – Les avantages? C'est que j'ai une voiture de fonction.
- – Il y a d'autres avantages?
- – (You like your job very much.)
- – J'aime beaucoup mon travail.
- – Quels sont les inconvénients de votre travail?
- – (Disadvantages? You work every Saturday.)
- – Les inconvénients? C'est que je travaille tous les samedis.
- – Et il y a d'autres inconvénients?
- – (You don't really have any bad points.)
- – Je n'ai pas vraiment d'inconvénients.

Activité 43

1 He talks about the importance of the physical working conditions. Are they noisy? Clean? He also mentions style of management: knowing how to find solutions together instead of having conflicts; knowing how to listen.

2 Yes, he makes most of the same points as the first interviewee. The first point he makes is that you need to enjoy your job (and he enjoys working in a high-tech aerospace industry). He then mentions the importance of inter-personal relations (*la qualité des relations entre les personnes… c'est un des éléments essentiels*). He does not mention the quality of the working environment.

Activité 44

1 An artistic touch, good physical health, a long apprenticeship.

2 Je suis **fleuriste** et je trouve que… enfin, c'est un métier très très très **passionnant**. Je suis très amoureuse de mon métier. On a un contact euh… avec la **nature** euh… vraiment exceptionnel. C'est un métier très très difficile **qui** demande un sens artistique, une bonne santé physique et…, mais, euh, ça compense euh… tous nos problèmes de manque de sommeil et tout ça quand on crée des bouquets. Qu'est-ce que je pourrais vous dire de ce métier? Que ça demande un long **apprentissage**, hein, que les employées arrivent en apprentissage et ça dure deux ans pour un CAP. Et après elles ont des emplois-qualifications, ou des stages **qui** durent à peu près deux, trois ans. Faut à peu près, pour avoir une bonne **maîtrise** de ce métier, entre sept et huit ans comme tous les **artisanats** euh, comme ça de, de fabrication, comme beaucoup, beaucoup de **métiers**.

Activité 46

1 (a) C'est un métier **que** j'aime beaucoup.

(b) C'est un métier **qui** a beaucoup d'avantages.

(c) Le pain **qu'**elle vend est très bon.

(d) Jacqueline est une femme **qui** aime beaucoup son travail.

(e) Colette est la femme **qui** travaille dans une écluse.

(f) C'est Colette **que** j'ai vue sur la vidéo.

(g) La camionnette **qu'**elle conduit appartient à l'entreprise.

(h) Claude Papin est un homme **qui** fait bien son travail.

(i) C'est quelqu'un **qui** travaille beaucoup.

(j) C'est surtout le style de direction **que** je déteste.

If you found you made quite a few mistakes or are still a little unsure about the distinction between *qui* and *que*, underline the subject of the verb that comes after *qui* or *que*. This should help you to spot the pattern.

2 (a) Le vin que Claude a produit est de très bonne qualité.

(b) J'ai rencontré un homme qui travaille à Paris.

(c) C'est un vin excellent que j'ai acheté à Angers.

(d) Le pompier qu'on a (*or* que nous avons) entendu sur la cassette s'appelle Alain.

(e) Les gens qui aiment faire la cuisine aiment souvent lire des livres de recettes.

(f) Les pieds-noirs sont les Français qui habitaient en Algérie avant 1962.

Activité 47

2 (a) Workers are more often off work when their company moves into a tall building.

(b) Drowsiness (*la somnolence*) and headaches (*les maux de tête*).

(c) No, these problems die down (*ces troubles s'estompent*).

(d) The young (*les jeunes*) and those who start their careers in high buildings.

Activité 48

1 (a) Elle les passe la semaine prochaine.

(b) Elle va à l'université le lundi, le mardi et le mercredi.

(c) Elle passe entre deux et cinq heures par jour à l'université.

(d) Elle va à l'école le jeudi, le vendredi et le samedi matin.

2 Liliane mentioned:

(a) faire les courses

(c) préparer les repas

(d) (faire) le ménage

(e) (faire) la lessive

3 (c)

4

Nombre d'enfants	Durée du congé-maternité
1 ou 2	3 mois
3 et plus	6 mois

Activité 49

– Vous avez droit à combien de semaines de vacances?

– (You're entitled to five weeks' holiday.)

– J'ai droit à cinq semaines de vacances.

– Et où est-ce que vous allez pendant les vacances d'été?

– (Sometimes you go to Spain, but you often go to France.)

– Quelquefois je vais en Espagne, mais je vais souvent en France.

– Est-ce que vous avez droit à une pause-café au travail?

– (Yes, you are entitled to 20 minutes' rest between ten thirty and eleven thirty.)

– Oui, j'ai droit à vingt minutes de repos entre dix heures et demie et onze heures et demie.

– Et à midi, qu'est-ce que vous faites?

– (You are entitled to an hour for lunch, but you normally take only 45 minutes.)

– J'ai droit à une heure pour le déjeuner, mais d'habitude je prends seulement quarante-cinq minutes.

– Les femmes en France ont droit à combien de congé de maternité?

– (They are entitled to three months' maternity leave for the first or second baby.)

– Elles ont droit à trois mois de congé de maternité pour le premier ou le deuxième enfant.

– Et pour le quatrième?

– (For the fourth child they are entitled to six months' maternity leave.)

– Pour le quatrième, elles ont droit à six mois de congé de maternité.

Activité 50

1 (a) Il va chercher les enfants et les ramène à la maison.

(b) Elle nourrit et baigne les enfants et les met en pyjama.

(c) Il regarde les infos à la télé.

2 (a) Share the housework (*partager les tâches ménagères*).

(b) Make the dinner (*préparer le dîner*).

(c) I come home (*je rentre*).

(d) Tidy the kitchen (*ranger la cuisine*).

(e) Pick up the children (*aller chercher les enfants*).